Life is *Beautiful*

Life is Beautiful

How a Lost Girl Became
a True, Confident Child of God

Sarah M. Johnson

New York

Life is *Beautiful*

How a Lost Girl Became a True, Confident Child of God

Published in New York, New York, by Morgan James Publishing. Morgan James and The Entrepreneurial Publisher are trademarks of Morgan James, LLC.
www.MorganJamesPublishing.com

The Morgan James Speakers Group can bring authors to your live event. For more information or to book an event visit The Morgan James Speakers Group at
www.TheMorganJamesSpeakersGroup.com.

A **free** eBook edition is available with the purchase of this print book.

CLEARLY PRINT YOUR NAME ABOVE IN UPPER CASE

Instructions to claim your free eBook edition:
1. Download the BitLit app for Android or iOS
2. Write your name in **UPPER CASE** on the line
3. Use the BitLit app to submit a photo
4. Download your eBook to any device

ISBN 978-1-63047-486-7 paperback
ISBN 978-1-63047-487-4 eBook
ISBN 978-1-63047-488-1 hardcover
Library of Congress Control Number:
2014919744

Cover Design by:
Rachel Lopez
www.r2cdesign.com

Interior Design by:
Bonnie Bushman
bonnie@caboodlegraphics.com

In an effort to support local communities and raise awareness and funds, Morgan James Publishing donates a percentage of all book sales for the life of each book to Habitat for Humanity Peninsula and Greater Williamsburg.

Get involved today, visit
www.MorganJamesBuilds.com

*To my dad and Zachary; a part of
my soul that will remain for eternity.*

To my mom, I love you.

*Finally, to Adam, Lillian, and William,
thank you for bringing out the best in me.*

Table of Contents

Chapter 1   The Crash   1
Chapter 2   The Secret   10
Chapter 3   Stranger in a Strange Land   20
Chapter 4   My Dad Comes Back   31
Chapter 5   Vicki   44
Chapter 6   Hospitals, Media & Coming Home   63
Chapter 7   Depression   87
Chapter 8   Falling   113
Chapter 9   Finding Pauline   128
Chapter 10   Lifting the Veil of Alcohol   140
Chapter 11   Finding Me   156

              Epilogue   179
              Acknowledgements   185
              About the Author   187

"When you forgive, you love, and when you love, God's light shines upon you."
—**Jon Krakauer**, Into the Wild

Chapter 1

The Crash

I remember all of the emotions, the trees whipping by, everything happening so fast, dad yelling, *Here we go,* and mom screaming, *Stop it.* I remember my brother Zachary looking back at me, his eyes bright with fear as I prayed *God please…*

I remember the sense of something coming; you know it's coming and wonder: will I live?

I remember the violence of the plane plowing into the ground as we attempted an emergency landing in a roughhewn field…*Boom, boom, boom…*and then nothing but an unnerving silence.

I don't know if I blacked out or merely paused with my eyes closed in the stillness of those first few moments. Awareness comes slowly. Then in a rushed breath of shock and revelation, *Thank God I'm alive.*

My eyes open to an eerily lit silence where sunlight and shadow intermingle, making it difficult to see into the new geography of the plane's interior. My head and body buzz. My mind trips on the dissonance of dangling upside down, held a few inches from the ceiling of the plane's cabin by my seatbelt.

Taking stock of my body, I notice that I peed my pants and there is a small cut on my left arm. Looking up, I see that one foot is missing its shoe. My eyes squint into bright sunlight that passes through a relatively large doorway next to me that was torn open.

The only noise to break the silence is the erratic popping of electricity; the final groans of a dying airplane.

I move my arms first and then my legs, which causes small shards of glass to fall from where they're lodged in my clothes and upturned seat. I tilt my head back toward the ceiling beneath me and it is covered in broken glass.

My hair dangles down away from my face, but the position of my body and the way sunlight cuts through the cabin makes it difficult to see much of the plane. In those few seconds I realize that I am okay and begin to think that maybe we are all okay; that the crash wasn't so bad.

I take a few deep breaths and reach down to my waist and tug on the seatbelt clasp. It releases and I tumble a foot or so down onto the ceiling. More by instinct than thought, I crawl on my hands and knees toward the large, incandescent gap in the plane's fuselage next to my seat.

The plane is a Cessna Caravan with a single propeller on its nose and wings attached to its roof rather than the underside of the fuselage. The interior is tight, but there is enough room for four rows of seats with a thin aisle running up the middle. Each row has three seats, one on the left and two across the aisle. My seat is on the left, across the aisle from my parents and toward the plane's tail.

I pull myself out through the doorway onto the underside of a wing and almost immediately a blast of intense, humid Guatemalan heat scorches my back. Shifting my body to see where we've crashed, my bare knees scrape on rivets fastening an aluminum skin onto the wing.

The world outside of the plane is punctuated by waves of late August heat and a landscape and flora that are nothing like my home in Wisconsin, nor anything I have ever seen at age 19. Near the plane, which came to rest at the edge of a field, is a row of palm trees and low, thick bushes. The dirt is baked brown and what grass there is looks more like tufts of straw. In the distance, the haze is etched with lush, green mountains. The far edge of the field, probably about 250 yards away, is bordered by thick tropical rainforest.

Turning to look toward the front of the plane I see the crumpled body of one of the pilots lying in the dirt about ten feet from me. There is a male and female pilot, but I can't tell which one of them I am looking at. I recognize the white uniform shirt, but his or her body is folded in half so that the pilot's legs are twisted around the head. The face is smashed and bloody making it completely unrecognizable.

My heart races and hands tremble as I realize that the persistent unnerving silence, no human voices whatsoever, means there are more bodies. I think of Zachary, mom and dad and stand to go back into the smashed, upturned body of the plane. The strong, raw odor of airplane fuel drifts around the fuselage in a thick invisible cloud.

My legs and body are weak and unsteady. My muscles shake so that I feel as if I'm shivering. It is hard to move as quickly as my mind screams that I should. I look into the plane through a mix of light and shadow. The interior is a maze of inverted seats and the only person I see is mom dangling upside down. Her face is scratched and bloody, and she is straining to undo the clasp on her seatbelt.

My silhouette in the sunlit doorway cuts across mom's face. She looks up at me. Her eyes are wide with panic, I've never seen her so afraid.

"Sarah! Help me! Sarah…Help me…

I climb into the plane and crawl to mom. It was a small space to begin with, but the altered configuration of the plane's cabin makes it even more claustrophobic and difficult to move around in. Her face is near my own as I reach past her hands to pull on the seatbelt's clasp. I tug expecting her to drop down as the seatbelt releases, but there is nothing.

"Please Sarah, please…" she cries.

"I'm trying mom…I'm trying…"

I pull the clasp again and again, but nothing. With each tug mom becomes more and more frantic.

"Sarah, help me, Sarah…" she pleads over and over.

The smell of gasoline is strong. The incessant pop of electricity as the plane's heart ground down makes me afraid the plane could explode at any moment.

I move my body to reach underneath her and I look across to where dad's seat should be. Instead, there is a flattened wall with one of his legs jutting out, motionless.

"Come on dad!…Let's go…Dad, dad…Please dad!…Let's go!…" but he is silent. It is hard to fully explain the sense of loss. I love him so very much and now he is so suddenly gone and incapable of helping me ever again.

"Sarah, we have to get out of here…"

"Okay mom, I'm trying…"

I tug on mom's seatbelt over and over, but I can't get it to let go. She is desperate for me to save her and I'm desperate to save her, but I can't.

I look down at dad's leg once more and feel the loneliness of the situation hit me. It sucks the wind out of my lungs and I can't think, I don't know what to do. This day began with a dreamlike quality that is now thoroughly a nightmare; one that I never imagined as a little girl lying in bed in the dark.

I'm alone in a destroyed plane with the crushed body of my father beside me. I need to save my mother, but nothing works and the smell of fuel grows stronger as electricity continues to erratically spark and pop around me. *Where is Zach, I need to find Zach.*

I pull my body back and look down toward the front of the plane, but I can't see past the second row of seats. Beyond those seats the plane looks like a crumpled piece of paper; it is a wall of wires, cabin and fuselage. On the other side of it are the pilot, two other passengers, and my brother.

"Sarah, Sarah, Please!" mom gasps in feverish bursts as she tugs on the belt with one hand and attempts to push her body upward to relieve some of the weight with the other.

Although I hear her, there is nothing I can do. Not only is the front of the plane completely collapsed on my brother and the others, but there is a fire and the flames are beginning to burn Liz as she emerges from unconsciousness.

We'd first met Liz and the other volunteers the night before for dinner and then we gathered that morning on the tarmac to leave Guatemala City for the small village of Sepamac in eastern Guatemala. The flight was only supposed to be about an hour and once we landed, our small crew was to begin building a school for the people of Sepamac. For me, this trip is a step away from failure in college, while for dad it is another stride in his path to redemption.

Liz is one of the leaders of our small group and I really only know a few scant details of her life. One is that she is in her late 30s and the other is that she is married with young children waiting for her at home.

I remember her excitement, which was shared by all twelve of us, as she entered the plane and took a seat directly in front of mine. Throughout our brief flight she explained what we would be doing, described the people we were to help, and did her best to make us feel comfortable in this new and very different place. She also shared that she was teaching her children Spanish and had flown around Mount Everest in a plane similar to the one we were in. It was amazing to me to hear all that she'd done and was working on in her life; far more than I expected I could ever do.

Now she's dangling upside down, held by her seatbelt, and will soon burn to death if I do nothing. I crawl through the broken glass littering the ceiling of the plane toward her.

"Sarah! Where are you going! Sarah come back!" mom pleads as I move away from her.

"I have to get Liz mom…"

Liz doesn't seem to recognize me. Her face is bloody and raw, she is in shock and confused. Fighting against the pain, she tries to speak, but all she can manage is to mumble incoherently and rock her head back and forth.

"Sarah, come back…"

"I can't, I can't help you right now mom…"

The fire is burning Liz's legs. I pull on her seatbelt, but it won't come undone. I move my body to gain more leverage and tug as hard as I can, but nothing happens. The fire is burning against my skin. No one else is coming to help. Other than my mother's frantic pleas and the popping of flame and electricity there are no other sounds of survivors or any other people. It is horribly quiet.

I feel like I am being enveloped by the strengthening fire and the destroyed interior of the plane. I turn slightly to my right and lying only a couple feet away is a member of our group. I don't know who it is. I can only see his motionless body from the neck down. His head disappears under a wall of wreckage.

The smell of fuel grows more pungent and a deep black smoke emanates from the fire. I turn to Liz and give her seatbelt one last try, but the fire is too hot and there is nothing I can do for her. I turn in the cramped space and go back to mom.

Again I tug and pull on the clasp to mom's seatbelt, but I just… *God, I can't do this, I can't do this on my own…* A voice inside my head said, *Be calm…*

"Mom, I have to get help. I can't do this," I say, working my way toward the doorway. "It'll be okay."

"Sarah, don't go…get me out…where are you going…Sarah…"

Out in the bright Guatemalan air, I'm once again hit by scorching tropical heat. I step toward the back of the plane and there is a shot of pain from my ankle. It doesn't feel broken, but the pain is distracting and slows me.

I limp past the twisted body of the pilot. Near the tail of the plane, I see that fuel is pouring out onto the ground from a large gash in what must be a fuel tank. I have no idea where I'm going or what I hope to find. My mind is simply focused on saving mom.

I come around the back of the plane and look up toward a row of palm trees. In the distance I see two dark skinned men pulling Dan, one of the volunteers I met the night before, away to safety. Dan is alive, but grimaces as they pull on his shoulders and drag him over the rough ground. His legs are twisted and one foot points out at an odd angle, they look lifeless as they drag across the rough ground.

I can't remember seeing or hearing the two men in the plane and I have no idea how they managed to get Dan out. I try to call out to them, *Come back…help me save mom*, but before I can gather my breath to yell there is a man standing beside me speaking Spanish.

He is very short, I feel like a giant next to him. He is wearing a white hat and shirt, jeans, cowboy boots and belt. I reach out and try to grasp his body with my hands and push him toward the plane, "My mom, my mom, you have to get my mom…"

I can see his wide brown eyes so clearly as he calmly says in heavily accented English,"No… nonono… no…" Behind me I hear mom screaming for her life, *Oh my God, mom is burning, mom is burning to death right now.*

I try to push him again, "Please, my mom, you have to help me get my mom," but he calmly says *No... nononon... no.* I am completely helpless as he gently, but insistently holding my arms, guides me away from the plane.

Mom is screaming, "Help me...please...Sarah, Sarah...help me..." as the man in the white hat sits me down on a dirt roadway lined by thick bushes. I'm about 200 feet from the plane and the flames are really coming. I can only imagine the pain of burning to death; knowing that your daughter just walked away from you.

I close my eyes to escape the image of it all. A hand touches my shoulder...and then another and another. I open my eyes. Standing around me are about twelve people; men, women and a few children. Each of them places a hand on me and begins to pray in what I think is Spanish. Their accent is different from anything I've ever heard before and some of the words don't seem to be Spanish.

"Sarah...please..."

I've never been touched or prayed for in that manner. I bow my head...

"Sarah..."

...and pray...

"Sarah…"

…and the plane explodes.

Chapter 2

The Secret

I've never been as angry with dad as I slam the phone down. I suspected he was up to something, but now I don't know what to do other than be angry. I look out the window of our log home in western Wisconsin. It's late January and I watch Zach as he shovels snow; his lean body working against the weight of it. The effort is written across his handsome face.

Dad is something of a mystery to me. He's a pleasant and friendly man. He works hard and is well respected for his work at Smyth Companies as a maintenance manager and for the furniture he makes in the small, brown-pole-barn woodshop behind our home.

He's predictable in his habits. He always wears suspenders that bulge around his modest belly. His daily uniform is jeans and button up shirts, although he often wears a Harley Davidson t-shirt in the summer. He has soft brown eyes and wears wire framed glasses. His greying hair falls easily across his forehead and there is something about his straggly beard that I find comforting.

Dad loves chocolate. In the middle of the night I hear him slide his feet down the stairs from his and mom's room, which is a loft above the living room, and then pad his way into our kitchen. I hear the clink of a jar filled with M&Ms as he puts it to his mouth and drinks them in. He also loves making us laugh and often pokes his tongue through a missing eye tooth in a way that makes Zach and me smile.

And of course there are the brown work boots laced all the way to the top—mid shin—with yellow laces and wool socks hanging loosely around the cuff. They represent that he is a man who has worked hard his entire life. Neither of my parents went to college, but they both know and appreciate the value of work and keeping a good home for Zach and me.

He's a creative man and this side of him comes out in his woodshop. He crafts what I would loosely describe as log furniture, which fits well with his lumberjack-like nature. They are sturdy, well-crafted pieces that he sells to our friends and family and to others on referral for extra cash.

He is also curious and always tinkering and creating small mechanical inventions or finding ways to improve a deer stand or build a car jack rather than pay money for either. If he can find a way to solve a problem and build it himself, he will.

I love dad and I'm proud of the work he does, his creativity and the effort he puts into it all, especially out back late at night in his woodshop.

I don't know that as he works away he's smoking meth.

❧※❧

Thursday, the night before the phone call, a large snowstorm passed through canceling school the next day. Mom left for her job at Kraft Foods very early that morning, which was her routine. Up around one or two and off to work until midday.

It was also her routine to call us each morning to make sure Zach and I are up and getting ready for school. On this particular morning she was more worried about dad.

"Sarah, is your dad home? Is he okay? He didn't come home last night," she said.

"No mom, I haven't seen him, but I'm sure he's fine."

"What if he crashed his car?"

"He's fine," I said. "We would have heard something."

❧❧

Despite all of his qualities, life with dad was defined more by his absence than his presence. Mom left early for work, dad a little while later. Most mornings, Zach and I woke to an empty house and dealt with making lunch and getting ready for school on our own. We would come home from school to our mom puttering around the house and making supper for the four of us, even though dad rarely made it home for dinner.

Some nights, we would wait and wait, but dad wouldn't come, so we put a plate in the oven to keep warm and the three of us ate without him.

Around eleven at night, sometimes later, rarely earlier, dad would roll in and I'd hear his footsteps pass through the house. He'd stop in the kitchen to eat alone, he always ate alone, then wander out to his woodshop. At about one in the morning he'd come back in and go to sleep to be up for work at five.

We didn't question that work was keeping him out so late. Working long hours seemed to be such a part of his character. Of course, it really wasn't just his work that kept him away. His absence from the routine of our family made it hard to truly know him. He was always off doing his own thing and we just accepted that it was all for us; to earn money and keep our family going. We trusted him. This is what life with him was like for nearly ten years.

Even family vacations followed a routine defined by dad's absence. There were trips to Florida, Las Vegas, cruises, and the Grand Canyon. On each, he managed to isolate himself.

"I'm tired," he would say, "I need some time on my own."

The three of us would leave him behind to explore and play.

At seventeen years old, I loved him, but I never put him on a pedestal or thought that I wanted to be like him someday. He was dad, but I couldn't say that I respected or admired him.

If I respected either of my parents, it was mom.

❧❧

After her panicked call asking if dad made it home, Zach and I set to shoveling the new snow.

The cold bit at my lips and nose and the air was still. We worked quietly through a well-worn routine. I didn't think much about dad's absence. Some excuse would come from him later and it would just be one more day when he had gone missing. He was a very good liar and manipulator, two qualities of a successful addict.

I heard the phone ringing and assumed it must be him. I plunged the shovel into a pile of snow and went inside. It took me a moment to pull my snow-covered boots off and the answering machine clicked on. I heard our brief message and then dad's voice, "April, I'm in jail…"

I picked up the phone, "How could you do this to your family? We trusted you…" and hung up on him.

❧❧

A few weeks before his arrest, the wall between his drug use and our family began to crumble. Despite his skills as a liar and manipulator, it was hard to perfectly hide his drug addiction.

After school one day, mom asked me to sit with her at the kitchen table.

"Sarah I found a black bag back in the woodshop …"

"Yeah…"

"…and it had had a pipe and some other stuff for using drugs in it." She had no idea what meth was, she'd heard of it, but never seen it in her life.

I was a junior in high school and played on the soccer team, but I wasn't so young or such a jock that I was naïve to the drugs that existed even in our small, remote town. However, I believed that these things happened to other people, other families. The thought of dad using hard drugs and bringing it into our home stung.

"Did you talk to dad about this?"

"I asked him about it and he said, 'Oh, it's a pipe for smoking meth, but it's just a friend's,' and that was all he would say."

"Mom, sober people do not hang out with meth users and why would he have this stuff out there if it was a friend's?"

"I don't know."

"Do you really believe that? Do you really think he would hide this stuff out back if it really was a friend's?"

One of mom's greatest qualities is a willingness to always trust and see the good in people. It's a great quality, but it got her into trouble.

I looked hard at mom. She looked away from me. She was worried, but she was also done talking about it. She wanted to believe dad and deny what I think she probably knew was true.

I wanted to believe dad too and I wanted to think that this was some dumb thing he'd done for a friend, but I couldn't go that far.

"This is my husband and I have to believe him," she said, getting up from the table. That was it.

※※※

A week later Zach, mom, and I were watching Oprah on TV after school. The show was about meth and Oprah showed some of the common paraphernalia.

"I found one of those pipe's in dad's hunting bag," Zach said.

Mom and I looked at each other.

"Do you think he is really doing this?" Zach asked.

"Don't worry about it Zach," I said. "Dad wouldn't do that."

He was only 15 and I didn't want this in Zach's head. It also seemed unreal to me that dad was doing something so stupid and reckless, that he was so dishonest. How could meth be part of my family? How could this man, who in every other way was a gentle and hard working person, fall into such a deep and dangerous hole?

I suppose, too, that I was hurt and wondered why I wasn't enough, why mom and Zach weren't enough, for him not to do this. I loved him so much, but it felt broken, gone.

I didn't confront him about it or speak to anyone else. Neither did mom. It wasn't our way to reach out to others.

Amery is a small town with little in it and only about 2,000 people who live there year-round. There are lots of nursing homes, churches and a few bars… A McDonald's came to town only a few years ago. I didn't see a black person until I went to high school; even then it was just one kid.

It was a big hunting community where kids took off school to hunt, but the rest of the year there was little for us to do. For a while we hung out at the movie theater, but that closed down so there was just a lot of loitering. Boredom naturally led to gossip and everybody seemed to know everybody else's business. I tried not to be a gossip, but when mom chose to socialize she went to visit family about an hour away— she didn't have friends, only family—where she'd tell stories on people… *Did you hear what so and so did?*…and that sort of thing.

My family lived about 20 miles outside of town. For a town and community defined by its rural nature, people viewed us as living out in the sticks. I'm not sure if being so removed made it hard for my parents to form social bonds or if it was just their nature, but except for a few friends they kept to themselves. I remember dragging mom to one of my soccer games only to see her sitting in a fold-up chair by herself. All the other parents sat together and chatted. Of course, dad was always somewhere else.

They were loners, which insulated them from being the object of gossip. However, it made them appear distant even to Zach and me. It was hard for us to reveal our emotions or have difficult conversations. There was love and arguments and shared moments, but never the ability to connect with our parents in a way that made confronting dad possible.

Until he got arrested.

※※

After hanging up on dad, the one phone call they let him make, his entire hidden life, the lies and manipulation, and his absence from our lives is clear. I'm angry that he could do this to his wife, to his children. I'm sickened that he took our love and loyalty and betrayed it all.

Before the truth came out, I looked up to dad, despite his absence, and believed that if we had more money he could be more present in our lives. I thought he was sacrificing for us and trading his time and energy for financial security. But now I know this isn't true. He's living a lie and betraying my trust and I realize that what's been important to him, more important than his family, is meth.

I want to put him in his place, but after the call there is nothing other than an empty anger. Now what? When you are so young and face such a tear to the very fabric of your family, what I thought our family to be, what do you do to pull it all back together?

Zach continues shoveling and I watch him for a moment. What will he think? What will he do? He is the steady person in our family, the one I can speak with and share. He is a young man, but this is beyond his calm and gentle way of easing my emotions. I don't know what to do with the hurt and the anger and I feel so overwhelmed by it and alone. I want to protect Zach and wonder if my mother, so unwilling to confront dad for so long, will even be able to stand up and manage this.

I pick up the phone and call her work number.

"Mom, dad's in jail. That's why he didn't come home last night. He's in jail"

"Why?"

"What else could it be for? Dad's been living with this secret and here it is."

Mom starts to cry. She expresses little else of her emotions or what she's thinking. I can hear the resignation in her voice. We knew there was a secret dad kept from us and now it is done, it is out. "Okay," she says. "See you when I get home."

Mom hangs up then calls the jail to tell dad he's on his own. He can bail himself out. I'm not sure if he stayed in jail that Friday night, an extra night, because he had to get bail money together or because he simply didn't want to come home. Maybe he was too afraid or needed time to think, but on Saturday he posted bail, got his truck out of impound and drove home.

Mom's running errands when dad comes home late that afternoon. I hear the front door open, feel a draft of cold air, and the door shuts firmly. Dad stomps his boots and takes them off. He glares at me as he walks through the living room. I give back as good as I get. He climbs the stairs to the bedroom slowly. Zach and I don't say a word. There's no door to their room. All we hear is his body settle into a couch in their room, and nothing else.

It's not long before mom comes home and sees dad's truck.

She walks past Zach and me briskly then up the stairs. She looks into their room. Dad is still sitting in the couch, in the dark.

"What's going on?" she asks.

"I was in jail for drugs."

"Yeah? No kidding. Clean up your act or we're gone." I'm surprised by her firmness. Zach looks at me, scared because he's never seen this either. Would mom actually throw dad out?

"I will."

They speak for a little while longer and work through mom's immediate anger.

"Ready to talk to Zach and Sarah?" mom says.

"Yeah, I guess so."

As they come downstairs, dad walks with his tail between his legs. He's a chastened man and I think he knows he's at the precipice of losing his family.

The two of them come into the living room and sit down.

"Friday night I was arrested when I tried to buy drugs," dad says.

"Was it meth?" I ask.

"Yeah, it was. But I want you guys to know I'm done… I'm done and I'm never going to do that stuff again"

"I knew you were doing meth," Zach says. "I found your pipe and some other stuff in your hunting bag and I knew you were doing that."

"I'm sorry Zach…"

"How'd you get involved with it in the first place?" I ask.

"It was Jim… I got into it with him."—Jim is a good and long-held friend; none of us had any idea he is smoking meth too—"But I'm never going to see or speak with him or any of those people again. I love you guys and I don't want to lose you. I'm done."

Zach and I ask a few more questions. Dad listens to each with his eyes on us, but as he speaks his head bows. His voice is thick and he struggles with each word. He seems tired of carrying the weight of it on his shoulders, or maybe just exasperated and weary.

Zach and I pause. Mom looks down at her hands. Her eyes are red and moist. Then dad shifts his weight and leans forward in his chair.

"You know Sarah, there's something I want to say to you. I'm really, really mad at you for hanging the phone up. I'm sitting in jail and you hang up on my one phone call… How could you do that to me?"

"How could I do that to you? Really, dad? That's what you deserved. You're mad at me? You're the one who needs to start sucking up, so dad please shut your mouth. You need to think about what you've done."

He looks away from me. He seems angry, ashamed and scared. I hate him for what he's done, the lies, the double life, all of it. I'm hurt that his family isn't enough, that he had to find comfort sucking on the end of a pipe full of meth.

"Look, I'm going to need your support," he says. "I'm going to quit, I'm never doing this again, but I'm going to need your love and support because I can't do this on my own."

"Are you going for treatment or something?" I ask.

"No, I don't need that...I'm not going to do that."

"I love you and I hope you do it," I say.

"I love you too dad," Zach says shifting his weight back into the couch.

Mom looks at dad, but doesn't say anything.

"I'm going to sleep," dad says, easing himself to his feet. He looks up the stairs to his room and I think it hits him that this will be his first night's sleep in ten years without his body filled with the residue of meth.

As he is walking toward the stairs Zach looks up at him, "Dad we'll be here no matter what."

Dad turns and looks at Zach. His eyes wince and his body seems to slump as the pain of it all rips into him, "Thanks Zach."

Chapter 3

Stranger in a
Strange Land

The sound of the explosion is incredibly loud, but within a few moments there is silence. A pall of black smoke rises from the plane and with it drifts away any hope that mom or Zach survived. *They're gone, my family is dead.*

The small circle of people, who so serenely prayed over me turn from the plane and lift me to my feet. I can't hear or feel anything other than an unbearable emptiness as these gentle hands guide me around a row of bushes and down a short, dirt pathway. I look back toward my family, but there is only smoke.

There is no echo of mom's screams. No sign of life. There is nothing, no human sound, just smoke.

Everything is strange and different. There are palm trees, jungle, dense green bushes, and in the distance, lush green mountains. I'm exhausted from trying to save Liz and mom. My body feels heavy and slow from the intense heat and humidity. I walk among a group of caring people, farmers from a nearby village, but I feel so out of place, so lost. I can't understand the conversation that is murmured around me and even though my body feels weak and diminished I stand well above these very kind, modest people. I am a lone white woman bobbing in a sea of brown. I am not drowning, but beyond my tired, slow steps, I'm doing very little to stay above water.

I can't think about anything other than mom, dad and Zachary ... all of them dead ... as I walk against a flow of people rushing toward the plane. There are people on bikes, riding scooters, running, holding knives and machetes. Many of them don't wear shirts and their skin is sweaty as they hurry to see if anyone can be saved. There is so much activity, so much noise, but the vibrations of it all pass by me unheard. My mind aches and my body is silent.

We reach the end of the dirt pathway and I sit down. The others remain standing, looking in the direction of the plane and saying very little. I pull my knees to my chest and bring my hands to my face and cover my eyes. All I feel is the echo of the burning plane and my ears reverberate with the lingering pain of mom's voice calling out to me. *Sarah, help me ... Sarah ...*

A woman comes and sits next to me. I barely notice her until she bumps my elbow to offer me a glass of water. My throat itches and I ache for water, but what she offers is discolored and looked as if it was drawn from a shallow well or stream. I know not to drink it, but I don't want to be rude in the face of such kindness. I let her hand me the glass and I take a few sips.

The woman runs her eyes down my legs and notices that one of my shoes is missing. I had a slight limp as we walked, which makes her think I must have injured that leg. Without a word, she reaches down and rips my pants to expose my leg up past my knee.

"Stop, stop," I say and she does. I look at my bare leg, how it is uninjured, slightly tan from wearing shorts all summer and laying out in a bathing suit. I remember dad's lifeless leg, and the discordant image of his boot, sock, and pale skin beneath his jeans jutting out from under the plane's collapsed interior.

I look up and my eyes wander off to the distance, past the mournful pall of smoke rising above the plane, to the mountains beyond. Clouds seemed to rise and flow like steam across them. I feel the heat; truly feel it burn into my skin. The air is thick and heavy with the scent of burning fuel. I am surrounded by people, lovely people who have been so generous, but I never felt more alone.

My family is dead and it is now my responsibility to get myself away from this newly hallowed field. *God, help me,* I pray, which offers me some strength.

I push my body up from the ground and with the modest amount of Spanish I know, I ask for a phone and if anyone can help me reach the U.S. Embassy. They look at me without saying a word. I feel my ears and the back of my neck become warm as I'm suddenly and acutely aware of how different I am from these people. Their silence also lends an awkwardness to the moment that makes me wonder if I have misspoke.

In my periphery I hear a husky, deep voice call my attention. I look toward its source and there is a man, much taller than the others, with a big build and huge mustache. He raises his phone and offers it to me.

"The embassy; how can I call the embassy?" I ask in Spanish. No one seems to know so I ask how I can dial out of the country, which the owner of the phone is able to show me.

The first person I think to call is my boyfriend Jacob. We met and fell for each other during my first semester of college the previous fall. My attraction and devotion to him mystified dad and Zach and frustrated them as they tried to pull me from him. It was my very first experience being on my own and Jacob had a peculiar charisma that often made me feel uncomfortable, but also drew me to him. There was something inescapable about being in his orbit.

I dial his number, but I can't get hold of him. Then I dial the only other number I can think of. My grandma, mom's mom, answers the phone.

"Hello."

"We were in a really bad accident grandma ... everyone's dead." Without saying a word she hands the phone to my grandpa.

"What's going on, what's going on?" he asks.

"We were in a plane crash and everyone died grandpa." As he hears the words, he lets out an anguished sob. My eyes burn with tears welling in them and I look into the expectant face of the man whose phone I've borrowed. I don't know how much this call costs and think it maybe is a fortune to him. I want to offer him money, but there isn't any in my pockets. *You're right dad,* runs through my head. *I'm no good with money.* "Grandpa, I have to go now, okay? I'll call you as soon as I can. I love you."

I hand the man his phone and look at him. I tell him I need to get away from here. I need to find my embassy or someone who can help me. After saying this, I begin to take greater notice of the people doing all they can to help not just me, but anyone in the plane. They have no idea who we are. We are so different, so foreign, yet they don't seem to care. This thing happened in their midst, and they work and risk their lives to try to save anyone they can. There is no questioning of whether we are good or bad people, if we are there to help or hurt. They just do what they can and offer so much compassion.

The day before, my family and I walked around Guatemala City. We were sightseeing and exploring before leaving for Sepamac to begin our work. Guatemala City is ancient and bisected by large tree lined boulevards and labyrinthine narrow streets that often lead to small plazas and outdoor markets. Within this mix of the old are modern galleries, theaters, restaurants, hotels, shops, and tall office buildings and apartments.

On many streets we passed heavily armed policemen patrolling and caught the attention of nearly every person. Everybody stared at us, everybody. We were tall and white easing our way through crowds of people speaking a different language, brown eyes and black hair, many of them five feet tall or less. I was 19 and had never felt so different, so uncomfortable.

And yet, in the most difficult moment of my life I am dependent on this small group of farmers. They can't be more different from me in their culture and physical appearance, but they are kind and gracious. They raced toward the burning plane to do what they could and risked themselves in the process. They gathered and prayed for me and the others and stood vigil as the flames consumed the bodies of the plane's passengers.

I look to the tall man who leant me his phone. "Please, I need to get help." He reaches out and gently holds my elbow, urging me to follow him and his wife. He speaks a little English, his wife only Spanish, which makes communicating difficult and frustrating, but I hear him say "hospital" so I follow. They bring me to a small, beat-up compact car. There are seats for the driver and passenger and then a small bench seat in the back for two people.

The man opens the driver's side door and pulls the seat forward so that I could climb into the back of the car. As I do so, his wife climbs into the other side of the backseat. A man I hadn't seen before, wearing a large white cowboy hat, eases his body into the passenger seat. The car's suspension, axles and struts, squeak as our bodies settle in. I can feel it gently rock as the tall man lowers himself into the driver's seat and starts the engine.

The man's wife is beautiful. She has long smooth black hair and wears long, dangling earrings. The features of her face and her skin are soft and gentle with an almond-like hue. She reaches up and brushes a strand of hair from her face and in her eyes I can see her sadness. The car starts to move and she reaches out and wraps an arm around me and holds me. I can't understand the words she speaks, but her tone is of a mother softly comforting a child. She breathes deeply and lightly strokes my forearm and plays with my hair. There is a warmth to her that eases my body and slows my breathing.

I can't believe this has happened, I think to myself as the well-worn car clatters along a dirt road through dense forest. Looking out my window and above the trees I can see the huge peak of a mountain that looks so close, but is maybe quite a distance away.

The road twists and turns and our bodies lean into each sharp curve as the driver speed to get us to the hospital. However, there are so many bumps that he suddenly brings the car almost to a stop rather than bounce over them. Once past, he accelerates as fast as he can, only to slow a few moments later to pick our way over another bump and then accelerate again.

As we race along, we pass through villages with small markets or squares surrounded by modest homes built mostly of four posts and then plywood or some other material for walls. Some of the buildings are quite colorful and I remember one shop where the front is completely open with its goods neatly displayed; the three remaining walls are painted a bright green.

Cows and other livestock wander the streets and we have to constantly slow and find our way around them or stop completely to let them pass. As we do so, people pause, eyebrows furrowed, noses wrinkled at the appearance of this small car packed with four people, one of them a young white woman held by the wife of the driver.

Once we are past these small villages, there are sometimes fields, but mostly I remember the forest and the mountains rising above. It all passes by my window as the aged car continually slows and then thrusts forward as we accelerate, skittering around sharp turns on a rutted dirt road cut through a thick mesh of jungle.

Despite the lurching of the car in what feels like a manic race to an unknown and remote hospital, my breathing eases and my heart calms. I notice how beautiful everything is. It is so green, palm trees everywhere, ferns laying a carpet underneath, emerald colored moss draping trees that reach up to form a sun speckled canopy, and all of it bounded by mountains mottled by rising tendrils of mist.

I bite my lower lip and think of mom. *Dear God …,* I begin, but can't find the words to speak to my higher power. I simply can't capture the dissonance of the beauty surrounding me and the horror of witnessing the death of my family.

We don't say much to each other as we drive. I am essentially in my own little world as the driver's wife comforts me. At one point I ask to borrow the phone again and the driver reaches into his pocket and passes it back to me. I dial my grandparents again, but this time my Uncle Terry answers the phone.

"Hello? Sarah? What's going on?"

"I'm the only survivor, everyone in the crash died." There is a pause before my uncle speaks again. I strain into the phone to hear above the noise of the jangling car, as the car caroms around sharp turns, slows and pitches forward again.

"How are you? Is everything okay?"

"I'm okay … I think…."

"Where are you?"

"I don't know. All I know is I am on my way to a hospital." I put the phone to my chest and ask the driver.

"We are near Zacapa," he says.

I put the phone to my ear and tell my uncle.

"Where is that? What part of Guatemala?"

"I don't know. I'll call you when I get there." I close the phone and hand it back to the driver. I feel guilty not having anything to offer these people who are giving me so much. I worry that they are using so much gas and I have no idea how much each call costs. My face burns red remembering the last argument with dad. Of course, it was about money.

Not long after hanging up the phone we see the beginnings of Zacapa, a small remote city in the southeastern corner of the country. I can't remember how long the entire ride took. It probably lasted about 30 minutes to an hour, but in my memory it feels like a much longer journey.

We drive into a roundabout and then to the top of a low hill and pull under a corrugated tin awning leading to a small entryway. The front of the hospital is baked white with a few windows. The glass in each of the windowpanes is frosted or tinted so that I can't see inside. There is a short cement ramp and metal guardrail leading to the entrance.

The car is surrounded by media as soon as we pull in. Overwhelmed by the cameras and faces leaning in to get a closer look at me, I sit in the car until the driver comes round and opens the door for me. This seems to cue the photographers and reporters to push even harder to get close to me. The driver does his best to hold them off, but as I climb out I am immediately surrounded. Camera lenses point at me, the snapping of each shutter sounds like a constant ticking and the noise of reporters yelling questions at me that I can't hear or understand converge into a disorienting din.

It is loud and chaotic. It is a confusion of people all trying to get to me … asking for my story. *What happened? What happened?* There is constant shoving and snapping of cameras. I am so angry. I have no idea how they were able to learn of the crash so quickly or reach the hospital well before I did. I feel so exposed … so vulnerable. I try to cover my eyes and face with my hands and want everyone to go away from me. *Stop taking pictures, stop speaking to me … let me through.*

Suddenly I am draped by a coat or small blanket and the driver wraps his arm around me and leads me to the hospital entrance. I can feel people pushing and still hear the noise of it all. The driver calls out to them in Spanish to make way and I feel the vibration of his chest as he speaks.

Then we enter the hospital. It is just silence.

I uncover my eyes and my heart sinks. I wasn't expecting an American style hospital, but I didn't expect this either. I am in a long corridor. The only light streams in from large windows along one side. The walls are painted a pale off-white with an equally as pale baby blue trim running along the floor. The paint is chipped throughout and near the floor there seems to be a series of pits where bits of plaster have been knocked free. The floor is coarse cement that is potted in places and looks as if it would be rough to walk on in bare feet. There are a few gurneys along the hallway that look aged, as if they have been through a war.

A nurse comes to us and asks me in Spanish to follow her. The man and his wife do their best to translate what she is saying. Mostly she just asks me to be calm and tells me everything is alright, but it isn't alright.

We follow her down the corridor passing a woman and two small children seated on a wooden bench. They stare at me as we pass and then we come to a set of red doors with the word *Emergencia* written in white letters. The nurse pushes them open to reveal an emergency room that is little more than the size of a bedroom.

There is room enough for a few gurneys, but otherwise it is a small room without any shelves or any supplies that I could see. The walls and floor were filthy and mottled with the blood of God knows how many other people coming through here. A handful of nurses and doctors working in the room looks up and stares at me for a moment when I walked in. They look so young, like kids.

The nurse edges me to a gurney to sit me down.

"I'm fine," I say, but she continues to tell me to be calm and that everything is alright. The man and his wife do their best to help me understand, but it is all so unreal and confusing. I start to become mad at her and want to tell her that no, everything is not okay.

The nurse asks me to turn around and as she does so she pushes my body with one hand so that my back is to her. I look and there is a huge needle in her other hand that she is about to jab into my butt.

"No way!" I say. "I'm fine. Please … no … all I need is some water, clean water, please."

The man and his wife start to translate. I look past them into the rest of the room and hear the double doors open. A gurney rushes by and as soon as I see that I stand up. The person on the gurney is covered by a blanket and groaning. I can see her legs and they are burned pitch black and blistered.

My eyes follow the curve of these horribly burned limbs and immediately the crash, the smell of it, the sight of it, the sound of my mother screaming, my father's disembodied leg, the knowledge that Zach is buried and crushed beneath a pile of debris and the emotion of it all wash over me in one long invidious draft of memory and sensation. I am overwhelmed and nervously rub the back of my neck as my eyes fill with tears.

The nurse reaches out to grab at me and pull me back.

"Be calm, everything is alright," she says in Spanish with the man and his wife translating nearly in unison.

I pull away and walk closer to the blackened remains of this poor woman's legs. My mouth is so dry and I remember a bitter taste that feels as if it burns my throat. The doctor and two nurses tending the woman look up. Their dark brown eyes betray their deep concern, but they say nothing as I inch closer.

The woman's face is covered, but I can't take my eyes off her legs. One foot pokes out from the blanket and my eyes widen. She barely moves. The only sound is an unbroken moan of pain.

The nurse reaches out for me as she asks once more for me to be calm. I brush her away without looking. The woman's foot is burned black and blistered, but I can tell that it is short and wide.

"Mom…is that you?"

"Oh Sarah…where's my best friend?"

"Mom…dad and Zach died."

Chapter 4

My Dad
Comes Back

*I*t is bitter cold the day after dad returns home from jail. It's Sunday and snow clings to nearly everything. What sun peeks through is mute and beaten down by winter.

The house is quiet as I wake up. Whatever level of emotional sharing that is going to happen is done. I come upstairs from my room in our basement and walk out to the kitchen where mom sits idly leafing through the Sunday coupon section of the newspaper. She looks tired and rubs the back of her neck as she glances through each page.

"Morning," she says. Her voice is flat and I doubt she got much sleep last night.

In the living room Zach is watching TV. He sits in a recliner with his legs pulled up to one side as he scoops milky cereal from a bowl into his mouth. Upstairs dad is rumbling around, angry at something.

Each footstep lands hard and heavy, as if he is marking out space for his mood today.

Even though it is morning, the world feels as if it's perpetually dark, locked in the too brief and often bleak days of January. The landscape represents a painter's palette of gray; from ash to slate to platinum. In such light and cold it takes very little to lead one from boredom to depression. This is why so many people try to put drugs or alcohol between the two, without much success.

Without the buffer of meth dad seems restless as he comes down the stairs from my parents' loft bedroom. "I could kill for some food. Sarah, put a pan on, I'm going to cook breakfast," he says. His eyes blink at irregular intervals and he scratches at his beard with his fingers. Every few moments he tugs on the whiskers at the end of his chin.

Walking through the kitchen he picks up his cigarettes. Mom silently grabs eggs from the refrigerator. Without another word he steps out onto the porch and in one smooth motion lights a cigarette and stares off into the distance.

This is what life is like with him, now the final dregs of meth work through his system. He's edgy and restless when he's awake, which isn't very often. He sleeps for nearly an entire week. He's angry at everything. His temper is volatile, but he tries to control it as best he can. Zach, mom and I walk on eggshells around him.

≫※≪

It feels surreal walking into school on Monday carrying the weight of my family's secret like some heavy stone. I have such a big secret and I can't trust anyone with it. At home, mom and dad have far surpassed any previous high point of emotional sharing and at school there simply isn't anyone to talk to, to open up to about my weekend and how painful it is.

This is where Zach and I fit together so well. He is a sensitive ear, an intent and conscious listener who indulges my emotions and responds with a mix of kindness and hard honesty. I feel I can talk with him about anything, but he can't mend everything.

In the wake of the arrest, mom and dad's relationship doesn't really change much. Dad persists at being angry at nearly everything and mom remains silent in the face of his hard moods. His arrest and feelings of guilt don't provide the spark for either of them to reach out for the other.

They love and depend upon each other in what I will come to learn is a very meaningful way, but as their daughter looking from the outside in, they appear to me as just surface people. I don't think I'm cruel. They've been through a lot in their lives and learned never to be emotionally vulnerable.

Dad grew up as the oldest of nine kids—five boys and four girls—in a Mormon family. Dad rarely talks about what it was like to grow up in such a household, but I know my grandparents were strict and dedicated to the teachings of the Book of Mormon.

I'm not sure if it was the harsh emotional intensity of their upbringing, genetics or some combination of the two, but the kids paid a price for it. Dad and some of his brothers fell into a world of depression. The most notable evidence was the suicide of dad's younger brother, Scott. I know Dad never really got over it.

Scott wasn't the last brother to die. In July of 2008, only a month before our plane crash, my uncle Bradley died suddenly of complications of the heart. Two years before that my uncle Brian died suddenly as well.

Death is not the only form of loss dad has suffered. Becky is my half-sister from dad's previous marriage and a virtual stranger to Zach and me. I don't know what caused the rift between them, but when she was 15—I was 8—Becky left our home to live with her boyfriend. Eventually she and Chad married and built a solid family for themselves, but we don't see them at Thanksgiving or Christmas and dad rarely, if ever, mentions her name.

I've always felt badly for her. First her mother abandoned her to live with dad, and now she is no longer in dad's life at all.

Mom's family presented its own challenges. She was raised by loving but strict, non-practicing Catholic parents, who were emotionally antiseptic. Feelings and emotions were rarely shared and most everything was swept under the rug; out of sight, out of mind.

The house was also filled with drinking to the point where nearly every family occasion devolved into some sort of drunken collision. Mom fell in with this family trait, but my aunt Vicki sought something different.

Vicki was born deaf in one ear and had very little hearing in the other. Most of her childhood was spent in a world of near silence with parents that never learned to communicate with her in sign language. As she grew older, Vicki made the decision not to drink and sought a life removed from her family. At one point she found a man to love and had three boys with him. However, her ability to live a completely independent life lasted only a short while.

By contrast, mom kept with her family even as she found the lack of intimacy stifling. She absorbed its traits even as she resented them, which made her a rather complicated person. Mom has probably been depressed for most of her life and has had her issues with alcohol. She also does not share her emotions easily, which makes her difficult to truly know.

But she really loves Zach and me and does a good job of showing that to us. She hugs us often and is easy with her affection, even though she never goes to our soccer or baseball games. Her affection is at home, away from other people, in isolation.

She also doesn't want us to be emotionally closed. If something bothers either one of us she wants to hear about it, even if it's hard. However it's always a one-way street. She wants to receive and never give. Her own emotions are always tamped down and hidden, which makes her desire for our openness feel uncomfortable and needy. I often find it difficult to open up to her.

That she so often doesn't know what to say or how to handle what she hears makes deep communication even harder. She has a desire to do better than was done to her, but doesn't know how to carry it off.

I imagine her life as a child was rather lonesome. For years her life with dad is no different. He is out of the picture doing his own thing, which must feel like a horrible rejection. So I suppose her outward affection toward us is as much about rejection and loneliness as it is about her love for us.

From an early age mom and dad also learned not to talk to outsiders about family. This means that dad's arrest is largely unnoticed by Amery's coterie of gossips. There also isn't any question that Zach and I will protect our family's privacy. It's not something we'd talk about, but there isn't anyone close enough to share such a secret with anyway.

By intention as much as situation, I'm forced to carry the truth of my dad like a heavy stone. I resent him deeply for it.

⫸⫷

Within a week or two the immediate effects of withdrawal fade and dad decides now is the time to be a better parent. However, he operates from a flawed parenting model.

Zach and I look up from the TV as he announces to mom, "I'm worried about the kids. I'm going to do more." It feels like a command out of frustration rather than a sympathetic appeal from a chastened husband trying to do better.

"Fine," mom says, "I've raised the kids for 15 years now so you can take over."

And thus, a new family dynamic is born that none of us is prepared for, or in the case of Zach and me, necessarily wants. Over the next few days and weeks dad follows his instincts and tries to enforce an idiosyncratic sense of orderliness born from his upbringing. He chafes if Zach and I display any lack of respect.

Within this muddle, dad does not trust us. He worries to the point of paranoia that we are falling into drugs and alcohol.

"Kids will be kids," is mom's mantra. "We can't control what they're gonna do; only influence them to make good decisions."

Of course, dad sees this as tantamount to chaos and surrender. "April, we can't just let them do whatever they want," he says

"Do you think I do that? Do you think that's really what I mean? Let them run around like they don't have parents?"

"Well, no …"

"They're good kids …"

"I know, but there's gotta be more than 'Kids will be kids' to keep them outta trouble. They need a firm hand."

"Like you got?"

"No…like I didn't get."

I hate his attempts to establish authority over us. This leads to power struggles and fights, frequently over inconsequential things. More often than not, Zach manages to fly under the radar and not upset the status quo while I throw rocks at it.

Many of our fights are over money. I work as a waitress and come home after a weekend shift with about $100 in my pocket. Within a few days, or even a day, I spend it on clothes, jewelry and things that he sees as frivolous.

"You can't waste money like that," he says.

I don't want to hear it from him and generally respond with a flip "Whatever."

Even simple things such as mom asking me to take out the trash spark fights.

"I'll do it later," I say and Mom shrugs assuming it will get done eventually.

However, dad sees this as rude and disrespectful.

"Get your butt off the couch and take out the trash," he says.

"Who are you to tell me to take out the trash?"

I haven't forgiven dad. I feel like I never got the apology from him that I deserve, that I need. He's never taken me aside and apologized. It just hasn't happened.

I want that so very badly from dad. I want him to explain his side of the story as a man to his daughter; to tell me how wrong he was and ask me to forgive him. I feel like it's his duty to at least give me a hug and say, "I'm sorry Sarah. I love you." That would be enough.

"I'm your father," he yells back at me.

"Whatever." He knows what that means.

"Who are you to talk to me like this?!"

Dad isn't the biggest man I know, but his hands, arms and body are strong and his muscles tighten as his temper swells. When I was a little girl he didn't often yell at me, but when he did it terrified me. It also hurt that he could be so angry with me.

As a 17-year-old I'm far more willful than my little girl self. I stand up to him and won't back down easily. It still hurts and scares me and I struggle to contain my emotions, but they often escape in tears of frustration.

"You don't have the right to tell me what to do."

"Why're you acting like this? You act like you're an equal in this house, but you aren't. You're nothing more than a spoiled, disrespectful little child!"

I fight with him not from the point of view of a teenager arguing with her parents, but as an equal, as a spouse fighting with a spouse. For dad, a man raised in a house where the roles of parents and kids were strictly defined as superiors talking to subordinates, standing up to him as an equal pushes him to the breaking point. Making it worse is the lingering effects of ten years of smoking meth: depression, anxiety, paranoia, excessive moods, and lack of sleep.

With his face crimson with anger, he turns to mom, "April you raised these kids to talk this way to us. It's your fault they're acting the way they are."

Mom rarely if ever says anything back. *What's the point*, she thinks, *he'll just keep winding up.* Her silence angers him off even more.

"Dang it Sarah, you don't always have to be such a pain!"

As his intensity escalates, I slip from resentment into frustration and then despair. The senselessness of the argument, the reality that I'm not going to receive the apology I long for is too much. With my emotions surging and tears streaming down my cheeks, there's nothing left but run off to my room. Escape is my last act of power and control.

"There she goes with the tears again," is his last stinging insult before going to the porch, his place of calm, to smoke a cigarette and think.

I throw my body down on the bed and let myself cry. Within a few moments Zach comes to me and places a box of tissues on the bed, "Are you okay?"

Zachary is a beautiful brother.

During these fights Zach acts like a stage director, in the wings, just out of site of the audience, trying to regain control over a lost and improvising actor. In hushed tones meant only for me he says, "Stop Sarah … Sarah, please just back down."

In my room he's always kind and gentle and speaks to me in a calm lecturing sort of way that I wish my parents would do.

"Sarah, you know how dad is. You have to learn to shut your mouth." Empathy rather than sympathy is Zachary's method. "You need to learn to back down, Sarah, because he is always going to hurt your feelings."

"Oh, I know," I cry.

Zach is stronger emotionally than me. Where I'm tearful and frustrated he's calm and contained. He doesn't let himself get pulled into power struggles. He exemplifies equanimity by allowing our parents' emotional detachment and dad's temper to pass by him like wind over calm waters.

I think he appreciates that I'm the emotional one in the family. He often says, "Sarah, you can cry for all of us when we need you to." Maybe I give him the space to be the modest little Buddha that he is.

By contrast, my emotions make dad uncomfortable, uneasy, and frustrated. "We can all count on Sarah to cry for us," he says dismissively. It hurts and he looks smaller in my eyes.

"Sarah, it is what it is with dad. I know it's hard, but just stop talking back all the time. I don't think it helps anything to just keep fighting when you see how angry he is. There just isn't anything to win."

Zach and I talk for 15 or 20 minutes then dad comes into my room. "Zach, I need to talk with Sarah."

As he sits beside me, I notice that his features are softer and his body far less taut. He picks an imaginary piece of lint from his jeans then reaches across his belly to scratch his forearm. "Sarah, I'm sorry I lost my temper. I feel badly about that."

"I'm sorry too, but why can't you be the bigger person?" I want him to control his temper and not say mean and hurtful things. I want him to be able to do that, but he never does. "Why can't you be the bigger person just once? Why do I have to fall apart like this every time? Why can't you just stop, stop for me?"

Looking down at his hands and rubbing one palm rather hard with his thumb he says, "But this is who I am."

"I want more than that."

≫≪

After the arrest, dad starts coming home for dinner at about 5:30 each evening. He stomps into the house unsure of what to do next or how to handle the foulness of his mood.

As time passes, the hold meth has on him slowly releases. He seems lighter, happier even. He eats more, indulges in chocolate with a relish that makes me laugh as he pours M&Ms into his mouth. He starts snacking on peanuts, chips and anything else he gets his hands on.

His body goes from the thin, dour figure of a meth addict to the portly, happier man of my memory.

He laughs more and starts asking about school. Zach isn't doing well so dad asks his teachers for weekly updates on all of Zach's assignments. Each night he sits down with Zach and helps with his homework. They look cute together trying to figure it all out.

And dad loves our cats, absolutely loves them … all four pile on top of him purring loudly as he sits back in the recliner scratching just behind their ears. He's in heaven and feels so loved by these animals.

Because he's around I'm so much more observant of dad and his habits. For so long he was an enigma, but he's involved now and has expectations for school, work, and how I live my life.

So the power struggles never end and follow a well-worn path: Yelling, tears, Zach comforting me, and dad apologizing, but demanding greater respect. Meanwhile, mom takes a softer approach with her kids-will-be-kids mantra. She's affectionate and even at 17, I can slip into bed with her and cuddle.

Mom and dad's detachment and isolation from the rest of the world remain. They simply are not PTA-type parents nor are they prone to socializing. Dinner parties and cookouts are few and far between.

School is no different. I work hard and receive good grades, but I don't really have close friends. The boys like me because I'm pretty, but I don't gravitate to any one boy or suffer through teen crushes like so many other girls. I'm aloof, but I allow casual friendships to form with some boys in school. I don't know what they think of me. Maybe I'm a tease or entertaining or something. Maybe they don't care or think they'll wear me down.

Girls are more complicated. There's tension, cattiness, and competition for and about everything. All pretty standard teen girl behavior, but I feel like a pariah. Maybe it's the number of male friends I have or maybe it's the hormonally powered high school rumor mill. I suppose it's a combination of the two.

I'd like to say I don't care, but I do. I just don't do anything about it. I have a few girlfriends, but they're older, mostly seniors, and our friendships lack any satisfying depth. They're fun, but I still feel lonely.

Zach is the only person in my world I talk to with any honesty or that satiates me emotionally. However, his friendship and love only go so far.

There never seems to be any real respite from the tension and stress that underscores life. I feel tautly coiled; like the world I inhabit spins far too fast. Like a merry-go-round you wish would stop for a moment just to catch your breath.

⋙⋘

I'm a junior and I take my first drink of alcohol on April 16, 2006, Easter Sunday, while sitting in a hot tub with two guys. Embarrassing. Yeah, I know. There's no fooling around, just two hard lemonades. For a moment the merry-go-round slows and my perpetual awkwardness dissolves. I feel fun and enjoy myself. Home and school are still filled with anxiety, but they are out of my head.

I begin drinking every weekend during school and then most nights during in the summer. I never black out, that doesn't happen until college. It's so much fun getting drunk and hanging out and lying to my parents. I discover this new version of myself; someone who's kind of cool, who's social and outgoing rather than isolated and shy. I'm my own person doing my own thing away from home as much as possible.

Drinking becomes the basis of my friendships with two older girls. They're on the verge of leaving for college in the fall, but alcohol facilitates an enduring sense of closeness. It's hard to think of them going off to more exciting lives while I remain muddled in little Amery. I don't want to let go.

※※

It's fall and I'm a senior. I long for something more than Amery and I find it with my girlfriends on their college campus. I drink in their dorm and at larger college parties. I lie to my parents and Zachary, slip away to the Twin Cities, and drink with people who are new to me, older and seem so much cooler, wiser and mature than anyone in Amery. Of course, there's a difference between actual maturity and feeling grown up. I pull away from my family and life in Amery. I become a different person in the Twin Cities.

I'm part of something and drinking helps me reach out and take it. It fills the space between boredom and depression, frustration and sadness. In my heart, though, I know I'm dishonest and selfish. I imagine dad felt this way for so long.

Meanwhile, dad's becoming a better man as he gains more distance on sobriety. The outside world slips from a cacophony of reds and oranges and blues into the deep gray/brown of late October. As dad slowly evolves into the man he is supposed to be, I'm too immersed in my own life to notice.

There are folktales in this part of the country of kids and even adults getting lost and freezing to death between the house and barn during severe snows. This is why they tie a rope between the house and barn, so they can find their way. Zachary is that rope for me, but I'm not interested in reaching out for it just yet.

"I know what you're doing," he says to me one day in early November. Obviously my lies aren't working on him.

"Zachary, you don't know anything."

"I know you're not going to Megan's. I know you're going to the Cities to party."

"Leave it alone Zach."

"I just know what you're doing," he says then walks away.

A week later mom and dad tell us Aunt Vicki is dying of cancer and coming to live with us. She'll die in our home.

Chapter 5

Vicki

eath came in an instant, without any forewarning for dad and Zach. Vicki was given eight to ten weeks.

Two years older than mom, she was diagnosed with cervical cancer in the mid-1990s, and beat it. Or at least she thought she had. Vicki walked away from her oncologist convinced that cancer was part of her past, not her future.

She avoided routine screenings and was lucky to have nearly ten healthy years, but eventually cancer found her again. She noticed ever-increasing pain in her abdomen and bleeding, which led her back to a doctor and then the oncologist. There wasn't much to say other than she had stage IV uterine cancer. Vicki is deaf, and I can't imagine what it must have been like to see those words, as they were signed to her by the hands of a hearing friend.

The cancer progressed too far for chemo or radiation to be effective and surgery was out of the question. Cancer owned her body now and there was nothing medical science could do for her other than offer palliative care. She sat quietly as all of this was signed to her and she could feel the two large tumors growing in her abdomen. Even still, the reality of it was hard for her to acknowledge. She insisted that she would somehow beat cancer again.

In her heart she knew she was dying, but it would take her some time to make peace with it.

She had friends, but none of them could care for her. She had family, but she didn't feel comfortable asking them. Vicki was alone, dying, and disabled. With nowhere to go she became a ward of the state.

For a time she was bounced from one hospital to another, never in one long enough to get comfortable. Finally, she was placed in a nursing home an hour-and-a-half from us, in Minnesota.

Vicki could be willful and dour, but she could also be kind and amusing. She enjoyed her friends and missed her children, but preferred to live alone. I suppose like many of the women of my family, she was rather complicated.

※※

With grandma and grandpa in tow, we go to the nursing home to visit her. As we file into her small room with one little window and a cinder block wall behind her bed, we can see she isn't the same. Vicki was always a big woman; tall and slightly overweight, now she looks withered and tired. She lost considerable weight and the skin on her body sags. I feel sad for her, but I also want to leave.

Vicki is totally deaf in her right ear, but with a hearing aid she has some hearing in her left. For a moment we stand around her bed not really saying much other than to wave and mouth hello to her. Grandma leans in to her left ear and loudly asks Vicki how she was doing.

"I'm fine, I guess."

Mom leans toward her good ear and said, "Do they treat you well here?"

"Huh?"

"Do they treat you well here?"

"It's okay."

We go on like this for a few more minutes. No one really saying anything of any consequence, just idle and awkward chit-chat. Then grandma says, "Well, I think it's time for us to go. You look tired."

No one says anything for a few moments. Vicki taps one hand on her chest and fidgets with a whorl of bed sheet with the other. She looks at mom, "I don't want to die here." Her eyes water and redden and her hand twists the sheet a bit harder. "I really don't want to die here."

Mom looks at dad. I guess communication for them occurs at the margins, in the glances, gestures and tones, more than words. "I know you don't," is about as much as mom can commit to in the moment.

The next day mom and dad ask Zachary and me to sit with them in the living room.

Mom clears her throat, "How do you feel about Vicki staying with us and dying here?"

"What?" I say. The thought of someone dying in our home seems so foreign, so out of character. Our home isn't a place where people come to die. I have school and friends as well. Mom and dad have work. Zach has his life. Where does a dying aunt fit?

"How are we going to care for a dying person?" I ask.

"Yeah, we don't know how to do this," Zach says. "What would we do?"

"We wouldn't be on our own. There would be hospice nurses to help us out," mom says.

"I don't know… Whose room would she die in?" Zach looks at me as if to say it won't be his, *You have the bigger room.*

"We'll have to figure those things out, but we can make it work," mom says.

"We have plenty of room and we'll make it work," dad adds. "I know this is a lot to ask of you guys, but this is important. Let's try it out and if you guys still don't like it we'll deal with it."

Dad stands up after he speaks and goes to his place on the deck to smoke. That's it. Conversation over.

I don't want Vicki to come to our home to die, but it is clear now that she will. She looked horrible in the nursing home. A catheter bag hung off a hook to the side of her bed. Her skin was pale and sallow. She lost a lot of her hair so that she had only thin wisps of it left. Her body was diminished as well as her spirit, though her stomach was distended by two large tumors so that she looked to be starved.

I don't want that or anything else that my imagination conjures as I think about her death. Crying out in pain over days or longer, a struggle to breathe, and a last horrifying fight for life after weeks of physical decay. I watched movies where people die of cancer, but it seems unreal to believe that they just fade away, that their bodies simply melt into clean sheets, a white world, and fading light.

At the same time, Vicki looked so sad and trapped. She was desperate for the end of her life to be more than the yellowed cinder block walls of an aged state-run nursing home; her last moments spent with nurses that are virtual strangers to her. Even as she assured us she would beat cancer, she wanted to maintain her dignity by not dying in that place. Mom and dad recognize this.

I wouldn't want to die there either.

When she comes into our home, her frame and figure covered only by a blanket and a thin robe, the truth of cancer is laid bare.

A hospice nurse edges her into our house in a wheelchair and brings her to the hospital bed we set up in half our living room. The nurse helps Vicki stand and ease herself into the bed. As she moves from chair to bed I see the silhouette of her body against the robe. She is so thin and frail, yet her stomach bulges out as if she is pregnant. I can't believe it, but I can see the outline of the two tumors growing in her abdomen.

Death seems so inevitable, but she continues to cling to her hope of survival.

The nurse helps Vicki settle herself and places the catheter bag on a hook near the end of the bed. It is about a quarter full and I can hear the yellow liquid slosh as it settles on the hook. The nurse speaks with Vicki as she works.

"How's that love?"

"That's okay."

"How much pain are you in?"

"I'm okay right now. When's my next pill?"

"Not for a couple of hours."

"Okay, I'll need it then."

"Sure…" and so on as she helps Vicki into our home and into our lives.

The nurse stays about an hour, but then it is time for her to go. We are on our own with Vicki.

"Vicki, would you like some music?" dad says into her left ear.

"Yes, I think I would," she says.

Dad runs upstairs and brings down a CD player and plugs it in. "What do you like?" he asks

"Elvis Presley." and that is how we begin to take care of her.

Over the next couple weeks, my parents change her catheter bag as it fills, clean her when she has a bowel movement, give her meds as she needs them, change the bed sheets, anything that needs to be done. Each day one or two hospice nurses come and spend about an hour with Vicki. There are the normal medical checks, vital signs and that sort of thing, but one of them, Maggie, has a sixth sense about the process of dying.

"She's doing well," Maggie says.

"What do you mean well?' mom asks.

"The tumors are growing and she's in pain, but she's okay…. She isn't ready yet." She sounds like a midwife for the dying.

Dad listens intently to every instruction, every comment; the whole while looking at Vicki, almost lost in thought. This is a project, a task, a job he has set himself to. He wants to be good at it, and he is.

I've never seen dad so gentle with anyone else in my life. One day I come home from school and he is sitting next to her rubbing her hands to make her feel good and ease her pain. He looks so kind and peaceful as he is doing this; lost in the moment and sensation of providing so much relief to another human being through such a simple act of caring.

"Are you okay Vicki?" he asks.

"Yes, this is nice. Thank you."

"We're here for you, Vicki."

I sit in the living room and listen. They are quiet for a few minutes, then dad asks, "How do you feel?"

"I'm okay, not much pain."

"No, I mean…. I know it's difficult to be happy, but are you okay? You know, do you feel loved? A little happier than in the nursing home?"

I can't believe it. *Do you feel loved… are you okay emotionally… are you happy… tell me about your emotions…* These are not words spoken by *my* dad.

These moments become normal in an abnormal way. Dad spends part of his day gently lifting Vicki so that he can rub her neck and back. The whole while talking to her, listening to music, calming her, helping ease the pain that seems to burn through her entire body, and trying to care for her emotionally. His words and movements seem so intuitive and natural around her, like he simply knows how to help lighten her burden, the weight of slowly dying.

I've never seen dad do anything like that before. He is coming around with Vicki and learning how to provide love and care. It is a side of him that he probably never knew he had.

It isn't just dad either. Mom finds a very soft, nurturing place within herself as well. She cares for Vicki with a sense of love and quiet calm that she hasn't been able to draw upon since Zach and I were much younger.

And my parents seem to discover each other in ways that life has never previously allowed. They split the shift during the day so that dad watches her while mom works and mom watches her while dad works. When they are together in the evening, they cooperate and engage with each other and Vicki in ways that I've never seen.

They both learn some sign language so they can speak with Vicki. They share changing out catheter bags or cleaning up after she moved her bowels. They share cooking for her and keeping her clean. They work together to change her sheets like they have been caring for the dying all their lives.

"Ready…? Okay, one … two … three … turn." They push Vicki to the right. "I got her … you pull out the cover sheet … okay … I got the pad … I got her. You lay it down. Here's the clean cover sheet … okay, one … two … three, turn." They ease her body to the left. "Pull the other side down … yeah, I got it…. Good? All set. Lay her down … gently. I know. Vicki are you okay, are you comfortable?"

Before Vicki they only lived their own separate lives, but now they have something important to share. They are going from strangers living in the same home to friends.

One of the kindest things I see mom and dad do is help Vicki reunite and say goodbye to her children. She has three boys that I don't think she has seen in ten years. I don't know why they became estranged. I guess Vicki is no more immune to emotional isolation than the rest of her family. I imagine her life has been just as difficult, if not more than, as mom's.

"April, I think we have to do something for her," dad says one evening in the kitchen.

"I know. I couldn't stand it if it was me. I'd have to see Sarah and Zachary." Then he says something that surprises and touches me deeply, "It would kill me if Becky wouldn't come to see me."

"Do you think they have any money to fly out?"

"I don't know." The next day dad speaks with Vicki about her kids and asks if he and mom can help fly them out to see her.

"That'd be nice," she says. They talk a bit more about the particulars and as dad walks away Vicki turns her head slightly. A single tear slides across her cheek and bleeds into the pillow.

Right away dad makes arrangements for them to fly out from Maryland to see their mom one last time. He even pays for their grandfather, who they live with, to come out too.

The last time I saw them I was five or so. Now, they stay with us for a couple of days and spend most of their time sitting with Vicki, signing to each other, we all share a meal, and sitting quietly in the same room with her.

"I'm sorry," Vicki says a few hours before they are to leave. Her boys look embarrassed, unsure of what to say.

"It's okay," the oldest one says. Afterwards, they sit and chat lightly, until it is time for them to leave to the airport.

As the boys leave, she promises she'll see them again soon, but the bulging tumors in her abdomen

tell a much different story. I can't imagine she actually maintains the cognitive dissonance to truly believe that her life is not near its end.

After her kids leave, Vicki slides down emotionally. She seems to disengage a bit from us and is quieter than usual. Mom and dad understand that having more people in the house probably would help her. Dad takes on the responsibility of inviting Vicki's friends to our home and arranging their visits. It's amazing. We start having people in our house; actual strangers coming into our house. And my parents host them and prepare dinner for them and care for Vicki as they visit.

We share Thanksgiving with Vicki and mom's family and then Christmas. Vicki has become part of our family and my parents continue to reach out to Vicki's friends to encourage them to come to our home. All the time, mom and dad are partners and friends sharing this experience, but at the center of it all is dad.

He lost people in the past; people who died suddenly without any chance to care for them or say goodbye. And now he has an opportunity to care for a person, to become close to that person, knowing she will soon die. It is bittersweet, but he begins to feel that he isn't such a bad person after all. He is capable of being very kind and caring for not just Vicki, but Zach and I.

He prepares us for Vicki's death in a calm and quiet manner. Dad does not hide the reality of her situation and how short her time is, but he does so in a way that feels caring and respectful to us.

"It's going to happen," he says. "She may seem really great right now, but she is going to die. It's going to be sad, but we will do this together. I'm proud of you guys. I think we've really helped her. We are the last pieces of her life and that's been really special."

※※※

When she came to live with us, the doctors predicted that Vicki had about eight to ten weeks to live. She's alive after eight. At first she does remarkably well. She brightens and becomes engaged with our family and seems to be happy, not just to be out of the nursing home, but to be among family. We enjoy her and beyond the efforts of our parents to care for her, Zach and I watch TV with her or listen to music and help keep her comfortable.

Early on dad tries to speak with Vicki about her funeral, but she won't have anything to do with it. She is going to beat this and be on her way before long. Dad presses her gently that she needs to talk about arrangements and the business of dying.

"Don't worry about the finances. We'll take care of everything," he says.

Vicki is adamant, "Thank you, no."

A week later, her body is starting to fail. She is quieter and her spark starts to fade. She eats a little less each day and is never really hungry. She becomes so thin that I can see the outline of her ribs through her shirt and when dad helps her up to rub her neck and back I can see the outline of each vertebra in her spine.

She starts throwing up after eating and her catheter bags aren't as full. Her eyes, which had been wide and curious, dim and her gaze looks at times confused and at others far away and wistful. It is clear she is slipping.

Finally, she asks dad to help her plan her funeral.

"Okay Vicki. Tell me what you want and don't worry about a thing," he says.

The two of them sit for a couple of hours talking about the music she wants played, how her body should be handled, the Bible verse she likes best, writing a letter to her children, her last wishes. It is all very sad, but dad handles it with care and in a business-like manner.

A few days later Maggie is at the house tending to Vicki. She asks general questions such as how much pain she is in and how Vicki feels as she takes her blood pressure and so on.

"I'm ready to go to the hospital and get my tumors removed," Vicki says. "I want to go to the hospital to get the tumors removed soon … they are getting so big it hurts to roll over you know."

Vicki looks at me, "I want to start driving and get my own place here in Amery too."

Maggie sits on the bed beside Vicki, "Vicki, the tumors have spread through your body and we can't get rid of them."

"I'll prove it to you. I'll be fine."

"Vicki, we have already talked to the doctors."

"Please."

"Okay, I can make another appointment for you, but let's see how it goes. Okay? If you start to feel better we'll make an appointment."

Vicki pulls her hands up to her chest then wipes away a tear with the back of one hand, "Okay."

The next day is Friday, the 11th of January. As on most Fridays, I slip out of the house that evening to go to a party. I get drunk and stay with a friend that night. The next morning my cell phone wakes me up.

"Sarah, it's mom."

"Yeah, mom."

"Your dad and I need to run errands and Zach has to go to work so we need you home. Okay?"

"Okay, fine." I wipe my eyes and feel the pain of a hangover pulse behind them. I pull my clothes on, brush my teeth and tell my friend I have to go.

"Whatever," she says from under her covers.

It is cold and overcast when I walk outside and there are a few inches of fresh snow. I start the car and get home just as my parents are getting ready to head out. Zach is looking for something before driving himself to work in the white Ford Escort that had once been Vicki's car. He loves that car. It is something of a rusty beater, but he cleaned it up so it looks nice. He also beefed up the sound system so you can hear the bass beats as he pulls up the driveway.

"Hi Vicki, how are you?" I say as I walk past her to the kitchen. Mom yells goodbye behind her as she and dad leave. The house is quiet except for Zach wandering around the living room.

"Zach," Vicki says, "make sure you drive extra safe. Sarah, I think you should go with him."

"Vicki I can't leave you alone. Zach is fine. Everything is fine." I lie down on the couch and close my eyes for a moment as Zach launches out the door with a quick goodbye.

About five minutes later my phone rings. "I skidded off the road and I'm stuck in the ditch."

"Come on Zach..." I rub my forehead. "Vicki, I have to go help Zach."

"I told him to be careful."

"I'll be back in a few minutes."

"I told him."

"Okay?"

"Okay..."

Zach wasn't going very fast. All that happened was a slow skid into some deep snow in a shallow drainage ditch that runs along the road. The low-slung front end of the Escort rests on packed snow so the tire treads can't gain any torque against the ground. This is the most common way to get stuck and takes just a little digging, rocking the car, and then a good push to get it moving and the tires back on solid ground.

I walk back into the house about 20 minutes later and say hi to Vicki. She doesn't say anything to me other than to quietly mumble to herself. Her eyes are fixed on some point just past my shoulder. Her voice is a low murmur and she seems to be speaking to someone just behind me.

"Vicki, are you okay?"

She doesn't respond other than to continue murmuring to whomever or whatever vision she is experiencing. She is very quiet and peaceful and does not seem bothered. There is a contentment or sense of serenity in her eyes and voice.

"Dad, I need you guys to come home right away," I say into my cell phone.

"What's going on?" dad asks.

"Vicki's acting really weird. I think she's hallucinating."

"Okay, we're on our way."

"I think she might die any minute."

"It's okay Sarah. Just sit with her and we'll be home."

By the time mom and dad get home Vicki has come out of it, but she knows what's happening. "Call mom and dad and the others, will you? I need to say my goodbyes."

"Okay," mom says as dad picks up the phone and calls my grandparents. When mom turns to look at me her eyes are red and moist.

Dad puts his hand on mom's shoulder and squeezes it gently, "Yeah, you guys need to come over here," he says into the phone. "Yeah, tell the others," and he hangs up the phone. "They're on their way Vicki."

"Okay … good."

Vicki slips in and out of lucidity. One moment she speaks to us softly or stares off in the distance. The next she speaks in whispers to people or hallucinations that seem to hover in some unfocused distance around us. After about 20 minutes or so she slips off to sleep.

Grandma and grandpa walk in a little while later and quietly ask how she is. Vicki looks peaceful, but there is a slight rasp to her breathing. Grandma goes to her and picks up Vicki's hand. Vicki wakes up looking worried.

"Where's my Jesus, where's my Jesus?" she says, asking to hold the small statuette that sits on the table beside her bed.

Grandma hands her the Jesus and Vicki clutches it to her chest. "I'm dying," she says.

"I know honey."

Before long the aunts and uncles come in and stand around Vicki. No one seems to know exactly what to say; sort of a pretty big test for such an emotionally withdrawn group of people.

Vicki drifts in and out. At times she wakes from sleep and seems surprised to see everyone. At others she speaks in hushed murmurs to the hallucinations that surround us. Watching her, it feels as if we are enveloped by the souls of those who will take Vicki to what lies next. Like us, they wait for the last remnants of her physical self to finally capitulate to the tumors that slowly choke her life away.

I am sad, but recognize there is a beauty to it all. My family has never been terribly religious, no church for the isolationists, but I feel there is more at work than the simple ceasing of physical life. I don't know my higher power, nor do I think it is possible to truly know God, but there is some unnamable presence in the room.

In the world of Judaism they have euphemisms such as HaShem, which means *The Name,* or Elohim, *The Power.* I don't now use the word God, but prefer to refer to this unknowable essence as my *Higher Power.* It is my Elohim, my HaShem. In the room with Vicki the pneuma of this power, of the word, helps ease her fear, helps her to say goodbye. It helps her body slowly release its grasp on her soul.

I have to go to work that night and tell my boss that Vicki will die very soon. He allows me to take the next few days off. That evening, Saturday, I don't go out with friends. I go straight home. Grandma, grandpa and the others have left. Mom and dad are sitting quietly with Vicki. The light in the room is dim and mom's hand rests on Vicki's.

"How is she?" I ask.

Mom looks up, but my dad turns to me, "She's still in and out, but she's been sleeping for a while now."

My muscles relax a bit. I have been worried I will come home and she would have passed. "What do you think?"

"You mean how much time?"

"Yeah."

"Not long. Maggie says another day or two...could be longer, but not long."

"Okay. Tell me if something happens."

Mom looks up at me, "We will honey." She touches Vicki so gently and in that moment I want to be held, to be comforted. Without the apparitions, the house feels so much lonelier.

I go downstairs to my room in the basement. I am tired, but not ready for sleep so I wiggle the mouse to my computer, but nothing, no spark of life from the screen. I have forgotten a guy is coming tomorrow to take a look at it. I lie down on my bed and sleep comes to me easily.

❧❧

The next morning I am terribly sick. I have chills, my head pounds and my stomach feels watery and sore. I stay in bed for a while hoping it will pass, but as the morning wears on I feel worse and worse. I decide I need at least some water and ibuprofen so I go upstairs to the kitchen. Mom is still sitting with Vicki and dad is up in their room napping. Zach has gone to work. I don't know why he didn't ask for the day off.

As I reach the kitchen, the doorbell rings and mom asks me to get it. "Maybe its grandma and grandpa," she says.

I open the door and standing on the porch is a thin wisp of a kid with a black tie, black pants and a white shirt. Behind him is a small car with *Geek Squad* painted in orange and black letters. He doesn't have a coat on and is shivering as he stands out in the cold holding only a black bag.

"Mom, it's the computer kid."

"Oh, okay. Let him in, I guess."

The kid looks at the hospital bed, but doesn't say anything. He quietly follows me to the back half of the living room where we kept the computer. It's next to Vicki's bed. He begins asking me questions about the computer. I feel horrible, but I sit with him and help him however I can.

I watch the kid click through one screen after another and race the cursor around the computer. He pulls up one dialogue box and then another until there is layers of windows popping up, text scrolling across them, and then disappearing. Watching him work makes me feel worse and all I want to do is lay my head down and sleep until it all goes away.

"I'm going downstairs," I say to mom. "I need to lay down, I'm not feeling well."

After about 30 minutes I wake to mom at the top of the steps, "Sarah, you should probably come up and talk with Vicki. She's worried about you."

I walk up the stairs and Vicki looks up to me. Her eyes are soft and seem to be filled with sleep. Her hands rest on her chest with Jesus tucked in her fingers.

"Are you okay?" she asks.

"No, I'm not feeling that well."

"That's okay. Go drink some water and go downstairs and rest. Everything will be fine."

I was just asleep in my room, is what I want to say, but instead, "Okay. I love you."

"I love you too."

The kid is still working away at the desk next to Vicki's bed. Windows and text boxes materialize then vanish. I walk to the kitchen and pour a glass of water from the tap and walk back downstairs.

Ten minutes later mom comes downstairs. "Honey, Vicki just died." Tears fill her eyes. "She's gone, she's really gone."

I walk upstairs and there is the kid, seated at the desk, staring at Vicki, completely unsure of what he's supposed to do.

Vicki looks peaceful, like she's asleep. "You may as well go," I say to the kid.

"Yeah, okay." Relief washes across his face.

Mom sits beside Vicki and cries. The kid does his best to pack his things and not knock anything over or bump into mom. I'm crying too. I've lost my aunt and am seeing my first dead person. I also understand that whatever influence she had over my parents, our family, may end. Mom and dad, all of us, may go back to living separate lives together, and that is truly depressing.

I tell the kid to come back the next day and walk with him to the door. He only glances in the direction of her bed; probably doesn't want me to see him looking.

"I have to go pick Zach up," dad says. "I'll call the funeral home when we get back."

Mom and I pull the covers up to Vicki's shoulders. Jesus is still clasped in her hands. I gently stroke her cheek with the soft skin of the back of my hand and say goodbye to her. She isn't cold yet and though her skin is a pale light blue, she looks as if she is in a deep sleep. She is the first dead body I have ever seen.

For the next few minutes, mom and I sit quietly with Vicki. Mom weeps lightly.

About 20 minutes later, Dad and Zach pull up in the driveway. The car doors shut and then I hear their heavy, male footsteps on the porch, the stomping of snowy shoes, and then the door opens. The two of them ease through the door. Dad's arm is wrapped around Zach's shoulders, holding him close as he cries harder than I've ever seen him cry.

They take off their coats and dad rubs the back of Zach's head. "Hey Zach, we knew this day was going to happen. She's in a better place now and she isn't suffering anymore, ya know?"

Zach nods his head and wipes his eyes with the back of his hand. "I just wish I could have been here."

"I know, it's okay to be sad."

Zach lays his head on dad's shoulder and reaches up and pulls him closer. "Why…?"

"It's a part of life, Zach. We knew this was going to happen when we brought her into our home, and today's the day."

Dad knows death. There is more death to come, but dad knows that feeling of losing someone close. He understands that there is no wishing it away. There is no honey-colored ending where everything is simply okay. It takes time to heal and he recognizes that it's a process that has to play itself out.

I think this is the first time he realizes that there is a role for him to play in helping people he loves heal. He is tender with Zach and gentle with me as we talk about Vicki and what it means to see her leave this world. This is Zach and my first experience with death so close to us, and it hurts.

I know this person. I love this person. I had a relationship with this person that became stronger as their body became frail and failed. It is an experience that neither Zach nor I have been through.

"I know it hurts," dad says as he holds Zach, "but it is very much a part of life and we'll get through it together, as a family."

❧※❧

The next day dad wakes up early and starts packing Vicki's stuff away in boxes. Mom wakes up, dresses and comes downstairs. When she sees dad, she starts to cry.

"Oh Roger, please don't do that. I'm not ready."

Dad stands up and walks to her and holds her.

"It's okay, April. I think we need to … I can take care of everything."

Later that week, at the funeral, mom starts crying during the service and walks out of the room. Dad follows her and holds her as she cries into his shoulder.

For so long we have been so angry and feel betrayed by what dad had done; the lies and drugs and living a life separate from us. But here he is caring for Vicki and then in our grief he cares for us. It shows me that people are stupid and fallible. We make mistakes, but those mistakes don't define who we are.

Dad isn't a meth user. He is just a troubled guy who turned to meth because it filled some hole in his spirit, even as it worked to ruin his body and took him from his family. I don't know why he did that. Dad lied, but he is not a liar. Dad isn't a meth user. He's just a guy who used meth.

And he is a really caring person. He sacrifices his work, his time, his house, his money to care for his sister-in-law because that's who my dad is. He is a loving and caring person, and I love dad for it.

I still have some anger, but after Vicki dies, the past becomes the past.

Chapter 6

Hospitals, Media & Coming Home

*B*efore the crash, mom is the kind of woman who loves feeling the sun's warmth on her skin. She adores summer and is most content landscaping and coaxing the flower beds around our home to life and then nurturing them as they grow.

When not tending her gardens, she manicures our lawn with a tenacity that makes me think she would mow every day if she could. I remember her plump body pushing our rattling, aged mower back and forth, across and around our small yard. The yard, flowers and flowering shrubs are a lush, green hued moat buffering our house from a forest of sugar maple, alder, ash, and oak peppered with dashes of white pine, hemlock and Norway spruce. A mix of light and dark greens, pine needles and broad leaves, it is beautiful on a sunny day.

This is how mom escapes her persistent loneliness and manages to find a sense of satisfied calm. It's a pleasant memory for me now. I remember her face ruddy and glowing from the sun. Her eyes are a bright Nordic blue and her arms tanned. White stripes cross her shoulders and peek out from behind the straps of her tank top and bra. Her brown hair is bleached by the sun and her hands are rough and creased with dirt. She is smiling.

※※

"Mom, Zach and dad died," I tell her as she lies on a gurney in the hospital in Zacapa.

Her face is swollen and blackened by smoke. Her hands are red and blistered and her jeans are completely burned off her body. The skin on her legs is seared pitch black and looks as if I could peel it off in large strips, like the skin of a charred hotdog.

"Both of them?" she asks.

"Both…"

She closes her eyes and turns her head away and weeps.

"Mom?" but she doesn't look at me.

A petite, dark skinned nurse of maybe 19 presses her body beside mine and reaches for mom's arm. She is wearing white scrubs and rests a flat metal tray on the side of mom's bed. In the tray is a butterfly needle with eight inches of narrow IV tubing connected to it. A saline bag with a much longer tube running from its bottom lies next to that.

The nurse's movements are short and jittery as she tears open an alcohol swab and turns mom's right arm to expose the inside crook of her elbow. Mom barely registers any awareness of what is happening. The nurse quickly cleans the skin and picks up the butterfly needle. She rubs her eyes with the back of her hand. Holding mom's arm still she pokes the needle into it.

"Unh…" Mom doesn't turn her head.

The nurse jabs the needle again.

"Ohh."

And again.

"Ohhh."

And again.

"Unnhhh…"

"Stop! You're hurting her!" I say. "Tie something around her arm so you can find a vein instead of just jabbing the needle into her!"

The nurse gives me a curt look, but puts the needle down and walks away.

"Mom, she's going to tie something around your arm, okay?" She barely moves.

The nurse returns with a length of rubber tubing and wraps it around mom's arm. After a couple more tries she finds the vein and sets the IV bag up.

Liz is only a few steps behind me lying in a gurney. Her hair and the features of her face are nearly burned away. Her nose is nothing more than a charred nub. What skin hasn't been scorched black is blistered and seared to an angry looking scarlet red. Burns run down her neck to her chest and disappear beneath a white cotton blanket lying over her body. Her breathing is raspy and between breaths a wispy, slow groan rises from her throat.

"Liz?" She opens her eyes. They are soft and rheumy.

"Sarah, what happened?"

I press one hand to my stomach as I step to the side of her gurney. There is a sweet, acrid, almost coppery scent floating above her body. Saliva swells into my mouth. "Liz, our airplane crashed in a field."

Liz's head rocks gently back and forth, "Oh no, God, oh no… Oh God no… Is everyone alright?"

"No Liz, we're the only survivors."

"Oh no… oh no. God how could you do this?" her tears melt into burned flesh.

As sorrow washes over Liz, the nurse tending mom's IV bag yells at me in a Spanish-laden accent, "Stop! Don't upset her!" Then she says something in Spanish that isn't very nice.

Another nurse, very young and wearing white scrubs, approaches and asks me to take the jewelry off mom and Liz. There is only a thin necklace on Liz. The pendant is burned so badly I can't tell what it is.

"Liz, I need to take your necklace off."

Her skin doesn't feel fleshy, but almost waxy, or like a soft plastic. Saliva swells in my mouth again, but I swallow it back down. She is so burned and I'm so terrified that I'm hurting her I move very slowly. I reach around her neck to undo the clasp and then gently slide the necklace off of her neck.

I look at her eyes, but there is very little behind them. They are barely open and fluttery. The compassion and brightness are gone, replaced by a soft, rheumy, distant stare. Her breathing rasps slowly and she whispers, *no…oh God…no…why God…*She is still alive, but her body is beyond pain.

Mom still looks away from me weeping lightly. I take what jewelry off her I can, but I don't dare pull at her wedding ring. I slide her wallet into my pocket. I can't imagine how much pain she is in. To my knowledge neither she nor Liz or Dan, the man I saw being dragged from the plane, has received pain medications.

Though Dan is not burned, his right leg, left ankle, and a couple ribs are broken; all of which must have been horribly painful. He is awake and coherent, but very quiet and seems to be in a dream-like trance.

The room is so small that I press my body against mom's gurney to stay out of the way of the young doctors and nurses as they care for Liz, mom and Dan. The walls and floor of the ER are cement and concrete block. There are no shelves, nothing but the gurneys, and everything is so dirty; a mix of blood splattered floor and filthy walls.

The man with the large hat and his affectionate wife who brought me to the hospital in their small car are gone. I don't know where, but they said they would be back. I stand by mom rubbing her shoulder and doing what I can to make her comfortable. Around me everyone speaks only Spanish.

One of the doctors motions to a nurse. In broken English he tells me they are taking mom and Liz to another room to clean and bandage their burns.

Mom looks at me, "Don't leave me, don't let them take me. I don't want to go with them."

"Mom, its okay. They're going to bandage you up and we'll be out of here in no time."

"Don't make me go ... don't make me go."

"Mom you have to go."

"I really don't want to go Sarah."

"Everything is going to be fine mom."

"Sarah, don't leave me again."

I know she has to go, but I don't want her to either.

"Dad and Zach are dead ... they're gone ... all I have left is you. I need you to live. I need you to do this so you can live. I can't be the only one of us to survive this."

Finding mom alive felt so very good. But we are in this strange place with people who don't speak our language, a culture so very different from that of Amery. The doctors and nurses are so young and so careless in how they touch and handle mom. To be stuck in this sparsely supplied hospital, its small and dirty rooms and hallways, feels like a nightmare. Mom is so badly burned, her legs scorched black and blistered, her life is still in jeopardy.

I'm afraid and feel so alone. I need her to survive this with me.

"Mom, I know this is horrible. I'm scared too, but please, they have to treat you."

Mom's eyes widen. She tries to reach out to me, but winces in pain, "Sarah, please don't leave me again."

"Mom, I have to, I have to let them take you. It'll be fine. You'll be okay."

Two nurses awkwardly maneuver Liz through the double doors that lead to the hallway. As the doors swing closed I think to myself that there really isn't a choice. Looking down at mom's body I can see the seam of her jeans burned into the blackened skin along the side of her leg like a horrid shadow or tattoo.

A nurse clicks the brake on mom's gurney with her foot and another nurse helps push mom to the door.

"Sarah, please."

"I can't."

Ever since that moment mom isn't the same. I left her dangling upside down in the airplane as she burned and now she is begging me not to leave her again, but I do. I have to.

❧〚

Mom is wheeled into another room and I sit on a bench in the hall.

Time passes slowly, but before long, the man with the wide brimmed hat and his wife return with a small bag of clothes for me. My t-shirt is dirty and smells of smoke. My pants are still damp from peeing in them during the crash and one leg is torn up to my thigh. A woman at the crash site thought my leg was hurt.

I go into a small bathroom and put the blue t-shirt on. I can barely button the khaki pants and they are too short.

Sitting back down on the bench I ask the man if I can borrow his phone again. I try calling my boyfriend Jacob, but there is no answer. "Jacob, where are you? I need you," I say into his voicemail.

I try grandma and grandpa again, but can't get through. I hand the phone back to the man and rest my elbows on my knees and lay my head in my hands and cry. The woman rubs my back and plays with my hair. She speaks softly in Spanish to console me. She is a lovely woman.

After a couple hours a nurse comes and signals it is time to leave. I stand and say goodbye to the man and his wife. She stands and holds me for a moment then whispers in my ear, *Te ama mi querida...Dios te ama demasiado.*

I turn as mom is wheeled into the hallway on a gurney. She is covered by a thin, white sheet that barely covers her chest and I can easily see that she is naked.

She mumbles and her head lists from side to side. A single intravenous line runs from her arm to an IV bag held by a male nurse as he helps a female nurse push the gurney out the door. Down the hall another gurney with Liz emerges, but before I can say anything to her, a doctor ushers me outside with mom.

The media come to life and begin to push and shove in around as two men load mom into an ambulance. It is an ambulance unlike any I've seen in the U.S. It is a minivan and the men have to lift mom up and angle her in through a sliding side door. Both nurses get in and kneel on either side of her. I climb in and sit on the floor of the van next to mom. The door slams shut and the van lurches forward, bouncing on its too-loose suspension.

The male nurse looks up at his female counterpart and says something in Spanish then smiles. She smiles back and replies. He laughs and says a few words. The female nurse titters. Her cheeks redden and her chin dips down a bit. She says something softly, just above the sound of the van's engine. Mom's body bounces as the ambulance slowly navigates through rough streets. She is naked and confused and scared. I can't believe the two nurses are flirting.

The ambulance wheels its way up toward an open field where a large helicopter waits for us. Four paramedics in orange jump suits, hiking boots, orange helmets with headlamps, and razor-type sunglasses jump from it and run to mom. They gently lift her to place a special cushioned board underneath her so she can be strapped into the helicopter. They're the first professional and well-equipped medical personnel to help us.

I climb into the helicopter after they strap mom down. I look down at her and her face is nothing but incoherent pain. Missing from the helicopter are dad and Zach. I can't believe I am leaving them behind, their burnt and misshapen bodies. It's too much for me.

In a few moments the engine throttles up and we lift slowly into the air. Time moves at a different, much faster pace. I remember the loud whine of the rotors as we speed over the jungle and then in what seem like only a few moments I see the outskirts of Guatemala City.

Seconds later we hover above a wide square of asphalt near a runway at La Aurora International Airport. Scattered below us are small groups of reporters and photographers watching us hover then slowly descend. As soon as we touch down they swarm the helicopter. I lean to mom and say, "Oh my gosh, here we go again."

One of the paramedics signals for me to climb out before they lift mom out. I do and instantly the media surround me. An orange-suited paramedic jumps out of the helicopter and wraps his arm around me and uses the other to push people away. Cameras flash as reporters wave their hands yelling *What happened? What happened?* Over and over.

We push through and suddenly there is a tall man with white hair,

 sunglasses, black pants, and white shirt tucked around his stout belly.

"Are you Sarah?" he says over the whine of the helicopters. He has a slight British accent.

I lift my head, "Thank heavens, yes, I am."

"I'm with the embassy and we're doing what we can to help you people."

"Thank you."

"We're all terribly sorry."

"Thank you."

"There's an ambulance waiting for you and your mom."

"Thank you."

"There'll be a woman from the embassy at the hospital to meet you."

"Oh, thank you." As suddenly as he appeared, he is gone.

My escort and I continue to move through the media. Like a tight school of fish they form and disperse and then reform around us as we move toward the ambulance. Mom is just behind us. She mumbles and tries to turn  her head from the cameras and reporters. Her naked body undulates under the thin sheet covering her, but photographers take photo after photo of her. To what end I don't know, but it feels cruel and my eyes well with tears.

"Will you stop?!" I yell.

Unfazed, the photographers snap away as the reporters repeat their incessant mantra, *What happened, what happened, what happened?*

Out of the din of male voices a woman asks, "Sarah? Is your name Sarah?"

I turn toward the voice and there is a female reporter. She is no more than five feet tall, dark skinned, tan skirt and white blouse. She is holding a pen and notebook.

"Yeah?" I say.

She pushes aside a male reporter and leans toward me, "Sarah, can you tell me what happened?"

"Translate for me and I'll tell you what happened."

"Si…Buena," and she climbs into the ambulance with mom and me.

※※

I can't tell if the scene at the airport or the streets of Guatemala City is more chaotic. Traffic seems to flow randomly at and around the ambulance as if everyone except the ambulance has the right of way.

We pick our way through the traffic slowly and mom, once again on the floor, bounces with every pothole and bump. The reporter asks me questions and I answer. Then I ask her to speak to one of the EMTs.

"How is my mom?"

"He says he doesn't know much. She is stable, but in very serious condition."

"Where are we going?"

"He says to Centro Médico." She looks at me. "It's one of the best hospitals in the City, very modern, well-equipped, he says."

"What's going to happen to her?"

"I don't know, he says."

The reporter asks me a few more questions about the crash, but it is late afternoon and I'm exhausted. She is polite, but persistent.

"I really don't have anything more for you," I say.

"Okay, thank you." We ride silently as the EMTs tend to mom. She moans with each lurch of the ambulance and I wish there is something we could do for her.

※※

At the hospital there is more media, more flashes and more questions and the young female reporter disappears into the evening. A handful of doctors and nurses walk with an EMT as he wheels mom into the hospital. They are swallowed by broad glass sliding doors. The other EMT takes my arm and guides me through the media and I feel like inexorable currents pull me forward.

Mom is whisked away down one hallway while a young nurse guides me down another. Mom disappears through a set of double doors and her fate is in the hands of another set of strangers. There is nothing I can do as I am carried by unseen currents.

It all feels like a dream. Mom, dad, Zach and I are particles moving in different paths, different orbits, to different ends. We are nothing more than dust gently blown by the unseen will of God.

I am led to an exam room and the nurse gestures for me to sit on the exam table. She says things in Spanish that I don't understand as she takes my blood pressure then temperature and pulse. She sits and punches numbers into a computer and a doctor walks in. She looks up and lists the numbers to him in Spanish. He nods and looks at me, "Sarah, right?"

"Yes."

"May I ask you to roll up your sleeve?" His English is only slightly inflected.

He gently removes the bandage covering my cut, but it bleeds as the gauze pulls at the scab.

"Does this hurt?"

"No, it's okay."

"I think you will have visitors soon."

"Who?"

"People from the church…a few others."

"Oh…"

"Of course, in Guatemala when we say *The Church* we mean the Catholic Church." He smiles.

"Okay."

There is a light tap on the door and the nurse opens it. An attractive woman in her mid-40s with dark shoulder length hair wearing beige pants and white blouse walks through. She has a clipboard with some papers clipped to it in one hand.

"Sarah?"

"Yes."

"Hi, my name's Jen. I'm from the embassy." Her voice is soft. "Are you okay?"

"Yeah, I think so."

"Physically she's fine," the doctor says as he pulls the last bit of gauze from my cut.

She pulls the clipboard to her chest and holds it with both hands. "Sarah, I'm really sorry. This is… well, it's really sad, but I suppose I don't have to tell you that. Everyone at the embassy is so sorry."

"Thank you."

"Can I ask you a few questions?"

"Yes."

With each question she pulls the clipboard away from her chest and then looks up.

"You're from Amery in Wisconsin?"

"Yes."

The next few questions are about the crash, my dad and Zach's full names, if I have contacted any family, and so on. She looks down at the clipboard again and pauses for a moment.

"Sarah, did your brother have braces?"

"No…" Tears wet my eyes. "Wait, is he burned that badly?"

"I'm sorry."

I wipe my eyes with the back of my hand. "He had braces once and then they got taken off, but then he had to have them put back on."

"Here," says the doctor handing me a tissue. He continues to clean the small cut. "You don't need stitches my dear. A butterfly bandage should be enough."

As he bandages the cut, Jen asks where I remember certain people sitting and what happened before the crash. I answer as best I can, but even though the crash was that morning, there are details I can't remember. What I describe is a highlights reel playing in my head. Over time, bits and pieces will come back to me, but that night I feel it more than remember it. It is fear, the concussion of slamming onto the ground and the plane flipping over. There is the terror of the fire, my dad's leg disappearing under crushed fuselage, and Zach's body hidden by the flattened nose section of the plane.

Her voice is soft and compassionate and I'm at ease speaking to her. She is a reassuring presence, but she is persistent with her questions because there are families waiting to learn about their wife, husband, son, or daughter.

❧※❧

The doctor finishes with the bandage and says I will be moved to a room in the hospital for the night.

"What about my mom?" I ask.

"We will get you to her as soon as we can, but she is being treated by a burns specialist and will spend the night in the ICU."

He leaves the room and the nurse asks me to wait a few minutes while she gets a wheelchair. Jen and I talk a bit more.

"What happens next?" I ask.

"We'll try and get all of you to hospitals in the U.S. where you can be treated near home. I believe we can move you and your mom and

Dan tomorrow morning, but Liz is in very critical condition so she'll have to wait."

"Okay."

"The embassy is arranging a plane for the morning."

"Okay." I'm too tired to say more.

The nurse returns and I step into the wheelchair. I could walk, but it's nice to be wheeled. She takes me to an elevator and Jen follows. When we reach the floor of my room the doors open and just a few feet down the hallway there are two priests holding their hands in front of them looking at me.

"They are here to pray with you," says the nurse.

Next to the priests two Guatemalan cops stand by the door to my room.

"The media is a bit too interested in talking with you," Jen says.

The nurse wheels me into the room followed by the priests. The guards remain outside. Though I am not Catholic I pray with the priests and accept their condolences. After they leave, a few more people from the embassy arrive to say how sorry they are. They also ask a few questions to prepare for mom and me to leave in the morning. Among the things they have to do is prepare emergency passports for us. Our regular passports burned in the plane.

Every now and again a lawyer or two asks to come in hoping to represent me in any litigation related to the crash. I'm tired and the guards fend them off.

By evening, the parade of visitors stops and I'm alone for the first time that day. The room is like any other hospital room. Bland beige walls with just a touch of color here and there, plastic water pitcher and plastic cups, bathroom near the entrance and a television hanging in a corner across from the bed.

I turn the TV on and immediately there is video of the burnt remnants of the plane. A Guatemalan CNN reporter atonally describes the scene in Spanish as images of the plane, then mom and me arriving at the hospital, pan across the screen. There is virtually nothing left of the plane other than the tail section and scorched ground.

I click the TV off. I can't watch it. I'm terrified of seeing a black body bag hauled from the plane.

A nurse walks in to take my blood pressure, temperature and heart rate.

"I want to see my mom."

"They're still working on her. I'll wake you up when you can see her," the nurse says softly. Her English is better than most of the other staff.

"Please put this on for the night," she says handing me a Johnny that had been draped across a chair by the bed. She leaves and I put it on and climb into bed and pull the covers up. In a moment or two she comes back in to make sure I'm comfortable and remind me where the nurse call button is.

As she leaves I ask her to turn off the lights. The lights of Guatemala City shine through the curtains. I close my eyes and think of Zach, his beautiful smile, and how much I wish I could talk to him. A light from a car or truck passes across the ceiling like a searchlight scanning an ecru fog for a lost life raft.

Zach, I miss you so much. I need you ... I don't know what to do. How do I live without you and dad? What if mom dies? How am I supposed to live without my family?

I'm lost and can't see a future without dad and Zach. How does someone move forward after such loss? What does that life look like and how am I ever going to get there?

I realize how much I need dad and I think about the argument we had over money a few days before leaving for Guatemala.

"You're careless with money," he said.

"It's my money."

"I don't care."

"I know what I'm doing."

"Sarah, you don't, you really don't."

My eyes welled and I felt overwhelmed by his anger.

"You always think you know everything, but look at where you are," he said. "You blew all your graduation money and all you have left to show for it is your loser boyfriend."

"How many times do I have to apologize to you?"

"Dang it Sarah, I don't want another meaningless apology. Get rid of that kid, move home and get your life together!"

Tears streamed down my face and I held my right hand up to him, "Stop, please stop."

His eyes widened and then he lowered his head.

"Let's start over Sarah. I'm your father and you're my daughter and we love each other."

"I know."

"I'm sorry, but I think we both want better from you."

"I'm trying dad."

"I know you are, I really do love you, ya know?"

"I do."

He pulled me in and hugged me. His arms were strong and he had an earthy scent; a mix of tobacco, wood dust, and pine pitch. It felt good to be held by him. It felt good too that he had been a bigger person. I never got the apology I needed, but his warmth and love was almost good enough.

"I love you too."

I wake in the middle of the night to the hum of Guatemala City. It reverberates softly through the room; a mix of cars, an occasional siren, the release of hydraulic breaks on a truck, every now and then a human voice. Otherwise, it is quiet.

I press the call button near my head and a few minutes later the nurse from earlier comes into my room.

"Can I see my mom? I need to see my mom."

"I'm sorry, but not yet. I'll wake you when you can." The nurse smiles, but I know she won't wake me up.

❧❧

The next morning a woman comes into my room with a tray of food. I pick at it, but I'm not very hungry. A new nurse comes in to take my blood pressure and all the rest.

"I need to see my mom."

"Let me check." She leaves and about 30 minutes later comes back with a wheelchair. I climb in and she wheels me to the ICU unit. It's early morning and much of the hospital is just coming to life. People are milling about, some rushing, some slowly walking and talking with a colleague. As I pass they all glance down at me and I feel like I have some mark on my body identifying me as *that* girl.

The ICU is dimly lit. Red and green lights are scattered throughout and everything whirs or beeps. There are no rooms, just curtain covered cubicles.

The nurse wheels me to one and pulls the curtain back. Mom is lying in a bed with an IV, blood oxygen meter, blood pressure cuff, and a few other things attached to her. Her legs are under a tent-like frame that holds a blanket above her burns. A clear catheter line runs from beneath the blanket into an empty bag held by a hook at the end of her bed. Her hands are wrapped in gauze. Her eyes are closed and her face looks so pale. Nothing like the plump, tanned mien of a woman who had so doggedly tended our flower plots and ensured the grass never grew too high.

"I don't want to wake her," I say.

"She's on a lot of medicine."

The nurse turns the chair and wheels me out of the ICU. As we near my room I glance in the room across the hall and there is Dan lying in bed. We see each other and he gives me a faint smile and thumbs up.

A little while later, a male nurse comes to change my bandage. He is wearing blue scrubs and speaks English in soft, short breaths. He is a very handsome man, dark features and fit, and is tender to the point of almost being affectionate as he removes the gauze and bandage from my arm.

"You will get through this," he says. "As time passes things will get better."

"I don't know, it's hard to imagine."

He looks up from my arm directly into my eyes. "Who did you lose?"

"My brother and dad."

His eyes are a deep, coffee brown. "I'm sorry. Right now it's hard, but things are going to get better for you. God saved you for a reason."

"I feel more like this is something God did to me."

"He loves you."

"I know."

"Always remember, your life was spared for a reason. You have a lot to accomplish in this world. You just don't realize it right now."

He tapes the gauze down and reaches into his pocket. In his hand is a folded piece of paper. "Here's my phone number and email. We'll talk, okay?"

"Okay."

He leaves and I put the paper on the table next to my bed.

Out in the hall, people pass by my room chatting in Spanish. Two new policemen guard my room. They are tall and imposing, but I can't see a weapon on them. Perhaps their guns are hidden.

I'm lonely so I climb out of bed and walk across the hall. The two policemen watch me silently as I knock on Dan's door.

"Come in," he says. Both of his legs are in casts, but he is smiling. I sit in a chair near his bed.

"Are you okay?" I ask.

"I'll be fine. I was just on the phone with my wife and kids. I can't believe I'll be seeing them later today, that we survived. It's really an amazing thing."

"It is incredible."

"I feel very lucky, but I'm terribly sorry for your loss."

"Thank you."

"So you didn't get much more than a cut? Is it bad?"

"No, just a small cut really."

"Sarah, you know you're a miracle?"

"Yeah, whatever."

"Don't you feel that it's a miracle?"

"I do. I feel very lucky that I'm unhurt and I thank God for that, but this is still hard."

"I know."

One of the guards pokes his head into Dan's room and holds his fingers to his ear and mouth as if his hand is a phone. The phone in my room is ringing so I thank Dan and rush to my room. When I pick up the receiver it's the voice of my friend Megan.

"Oh my gosh, are you okay?"

For what feels like the millionth time, I tell her I'm fine and then briefly what happened. It is good to hear her voice, very good, but I am too worried about mom and what is going to happen to us today to have much of a conversation. I tell her that I think I'll be home later and that I will call her then.

Almost as soon as I hang up the phone, a few more people related to the local Catholic Church come in. They are carrying a care package filled with toothpaste, candy, shampoo, slippers, and so on.

Then the man who drove me to the first hospital comes in with his wife. He carries his hat in his hands and the woman walks to my bed and hugs me lightly. He asks how I am doing in stilted English and if mom is okay. "Things should be okay," I tell him.

Then the he furrows his brow and says, "You are a miracle. It is a miracle, no?"

"I don't know, but thank you."

The phone rings again. It's grandma and grandpa. They ask how I am and if there is any news of mom. I tell them all that I know, but I feel awkward speaking on the phone while the man, his wife and the church group are in the room looking at me.

I tell grandma and grandpa I love them and that we'll be home later that day, I hope. I hang up the phone and thank the man and his wife for all that they have done. She hugs me and whispers, *Que te vaya bien.*

"Gracias, thank you for everything." They walk out with the church group and that is the last time I have seen them.

The rest of the day is much of the same. Every so often a nurse checks my pulse and so on and I ask her when are we leaving. "Soon," is all they say, but it isn't until three in the afternoon when Jen from the embassy walks in, clipboard in hand.

"Ready to go?"

"Yeah, where to?"

"Home. You're going home and your mom is being transferred to Hennepin County Medical Center in Minneapolis."

"What about dad and Zach?"

Jen looks down to her right, like something landed next to her foot then up to me. "We'll get them home, we really will, but, uh, I'll let you know as soon as I can when we figure things out, I really will."

"Okay."

"I'll give you a few minutes to get dressed. Take your time, no hurry."

I put the t-shirt and too-tight pants back on and pack up the care package given to me by the church group. On the table next to my bed is the piece of paper the male nurse handed to me. I put it in my pocket.

Soon a nurse is wheeling me down a hallway toward the ICU and Jen is walking beside me.

"How's Liz?" I ask.

"Oh, you haven't heard? I'm sorry, but Liz died last night."

A rush of heat rises from my heart to my face and I begin to sob. "Why?"

"Her body was too badly burned. There was nothing that could be done. I'm sorry."

Jen is quiet the rest of the walk and I work to pull myself together for mom. The nurse parks me just outside the entrance to the ICU and Jen stands next to me with her hand on my shoulder.

A pair of nurses with a doctor walking a step or two behind them push mom from the ICU. Her eyes are open, but they are flat and glassy.

"Sarah," she sighs.

"It's me, mom, we're going home."

An IV sways on a hook above her head and clear, soft tubing with two air vents for each nostril wraps around her head.

"How are we getting home?"

"Flying, mom."

She looks forward and closes her eyes. A gauze wrapped hand taps lightly on the bed.

After a few moments they wheel us to a side entrance of the hospital where an ambulance waits. This ambulance is nothing like the vans of yesterday. It's a modern, box-like structure with plenty of room for mom, the doctor, and me. Two American EMTs—I assume they are with the medical team we will travel home with—begin to lift mom and place her in the back.

Down the block, a few reporters and photographers notice us. They move toward us and before long the remainder of the crowd of reporters and camera people swarm around us. Cameras flash and questions are shouted at us. I duck away and Jen places her clipboard in front of my face.

However, I'm not the focus of the photographers. They push their cameras up as far as the straps would let them to take pictures of mom. At first they capture the EMTs loading her and then they snap away as she lies in the back of the ambulance. She is barely conscious and looks dead. Without a word, I climb into the back of the ambulance, followed by Jen and the doctor.

One of the EMTs slams the door shut and climbs into the passenger seat. The photographers hold their cameras to the back windows and pop away at us.

Once again we meander through traffic in Guatemala City. It is a confusion of horns, bikes, and motorcycles. Women dressed in bright colors, men with hard faces, and curious children walking slowly past outdoor shops covered by bright canopies. All of it, cars, trucks, cabs, and people are flowing around us.

At the airport, we pass through a gate and drive to a small jet. The sound and smell of aircraft rushes through me as I step out of the ambulance. The American EMTs walk deliberately toward the back of the ambulance.

"I'm fine," I say as one approaches me. He nods and the two of them wait as the EMTs lift mom from the ambulance.

"She's your mom, right?"

"Yeah."

"We'll take good care of her." He looks at the other EMT, "Let's get her stabilized in the plane and we'll do vitals and check bandages." The remainder of their conversation is a jumble of medical terms.

Waiting by the ramp into the plane are two pilots. Both hold their hands behind them, shoulders straight, their mirrored sunglasses reflect the afternoon sun.

As the EMTs wheel mom to the plane, she comes out of her trance, "Are you going to get us there safe?"

One of the pilots, a muscular man with shaved head and blond eyebrows, steps forward, "Ma'am, I'm flying this jet and I'm the best there is. Nobody better. So yes, you are very safe with me."

"You sure?"

"Yes ma'am. You'll be home safe and sound. I promise."

Then mom is lifted into the plane. I start toward the steps when Jen says, "Sarah." I turn and in her hand is dad's wedding ring. "I thought you would want this."

Tears fill my eyes and I wipe them away, "Thank you … thanks for everything."

Then I step up the ramp and enter the plane.

The interior is tight, but it feels okay. I sit down and look out the window. Jen is standing looking at the plane. The EMTs sit in their seats and buckle. Jen walks to a car that had followed us and climbs in the back and it rolls slowly away.

The engine throttles up and the plane moves forward slowly. The sun is bright and a few clouds drift across the sky. The nose of the plane points down the runway, I squeeze dad's ring in my hand, the engines rev and we slip from the ground into the air, up, up, and up.

A little more than 24 hours before I'd been on that same runway, in this same space above the ground twisting upward. Mom sat beside me, dad on the other side of her. Zach talked with one of our new crew of volunteers and I looked nervously out the plane's window. I believed the depression, loneliness, drinking, Jacob, and the failure that had been college were behind me.

I looked down as our small plane of volunteers climbed higher into the sky and watched a large truck get ever smaller. I realized how truly little and powerless we are. The truck became so tiny that it seemed as if I could reach down and tip it over with a finger. I saw that we are dust being blown by spiritual winds. In that moment I understood how connected I am to my higher power.

The propeller droned as we climbed even higher. I looked at Zach and he smiled back, the excitement of the moment written across his beautiful face. The sky was so blue and we drifted above scattered clouds casting slow shadows on the ground. We were between heaven and earth, above a vast, green canvas of jungle and scattered towns and villages. Earth felt as if it were some giant snow globe held in the loving hands of God. We are His to look at whenever He wants; our lives are His to cast in myriad directions as He sees fit. The world seemed so beautiful and life so peaceful. An overwhelming sense of warmth coursed throughout my body.

This was the second time in my life that I felt God moving through me in an intimate way, unique from the warmth of prayer.

Then there was smoke, a shudder. The engine sputtered and quit.

"It's okay, the pilots are trained for this," Liz said with one hand tightly grasping the back of the seat in front of her.

Then from near Zach, "We're dead."

Chapter 7

Depression

A few hours after Vicki dies, two men from the funeral home that dad found for her come and pack her body in a black bag and wheel her away. A few days later a couple of hospice workers arrive and pack up the hospital bed and the medical equipment that had made her final days easier.

Dad's planning for Vicki's funeral goes off with the same concise efficiency. We bury Vicki close to my grandparents' house. It's cold, but Mom's side of the family is in full force to say goodbye to Vicki. After the service there is drinking, adults talking, kids running around, more drinking and then they disperse into the night and it's over.

But not really. We are left with a home that feels too quiet and there is a sense of emptiness, someone is missing, and it is hard to adjust. The only tangible artifact of her life is our sadness and the sense that Vicki is not where she should be.

And yet, life is an unstoppable rhythm. Weekdays are school and homework. Loneliness remains, though it is diminished by weekend parties and drinking. I'm at the peak of teenage obtuseness and self-referential thinking, but I still manage to notice subtle changes in mom and dad's relationship. There's a mislaid closeness that slowly returns. A long dormant friendship is rekindled. Dad practices redemption through kindness.

☙❧

A couple weeks later Grandpa Jensen calls. There's nothing unusual about the call other than the length of it and that at one point dad carries the phone into the kitchen and speaks softly to his father.

When he hangs up he walks into the living room, "Zach, how do you feel about going to Kenya?"

"Africa?"

"Yeah, Africa. Your grandfather wants all of the men on our side of the family to go to Africa with him on some sort of humanitarian mission."

"What are we going to do?"

"Not sure yet, but build something to help support a small village."

"When do we go?"

"This summer."

Dad is captivated by the thought of traveling to Africa and dives into this humanitarian mission with a passionate enthusiasm I've rarely

seen in him. His energy infects Zach and thoughts of Kenya become an indefatigable point of connection for them.

☙❧

In February, there is an acceptance letter for me from the University of Minnesota in Duluth. College is not the first option for my family, only a few cousins have gone. Duluth wasn't my first choice, St. Catherine University in Minneapolis-St. Paul was, but it didn't work out. I'm still very proud to get into Duluth. It's college and I'm going.

When I show her the letter mom asks, "Are you sure this is what you want?" Her life is that of a working class woman. High school provides the basic tools for the job or series of jobs you'll have once you graduate. Beyond that, education is something you do as a personal do-it-yourself project. It's a simple formula and one passed down from one generation to the next in her family: Go as far as you can in high school, get a job, and make your money.

"Yes mom, I know this is what I want."

"Do you even know what you want to do?"

"I'm thinking about something like psychology, I think ... I don't know. I have time to think about it."

"Wouldn't you be better off staying near home and working? Maybe you could go after a while?"

"Mom, I'll have a better life if I go to college."

"I don't know honey; seems like a lot of money just to spend time with a bunch of brainy, over-privileged kids." Her image of college is born of movies and caricatures. "Are you even going to like it?"

"Don't worry. I can handle it and I'll make a decent living after I graduate."

"It's more than two hours away."

"I can handle it."

Where mom is apprehensive, dad is supportive. "I know you can do this. You'll be fine," he says when I show him the letter and tell him this is where I want to go to college. He understands the challenges, especially for a girl like me, unused to being away from home, but he also recognizes the benefits.

His way is a gentle persuasion and encouragement, sometimes in direct opposition to mom's worries. He takes me by the hand and helps me find my way through the maze of financial aid forms, registration papers, dormitory questionnaires, signing up for classes, selecting a major; the business of going to college.

Underlying all of his actions is a sense of pride. He is proud to be able to do this for his daughter. If I'm the first of my family to go, he's the first parent of his family to send a child to college. And he is proud of me. These words are unspoken, but self-evident.

≫※≪

In June, there is graduation, followed soon after by Dad and Zach's trip to Kenya. Upon their return, I hear their feet land heavily on the steps, and they seem to burst through the door. I'm so happy to have them both home, especially my lovely, confidante Zach.

"It was amazing," dad says after they settle in.

"Well, I did get malaria," Zach says.

"What!?" says mom holding her hands to her mouth.

"He's okay," dad says looking at Zach.

"Yeah, I'm okay now, but it was really amazing there," says Zach.

Dad takes over the story from Zach and tells mom and me everything they did and how it felt to be so far from home and to be in Africa. Africa for goodness sakes! My dad and Zach, the two boys from Amery, Wisconsin. I'm proud of them both.

As I watch dad talk, I can tell that his soul is renewed. He is not the same man who called in the cold of winter to say he'd been arrested. He is someone else now.

"I've never felt as alive as I did in Kenya," he says. "After spending so much of my life taking, I want to do something different. I wanna do more of this, to give back, and I want you all with me. I want all of us to do this, to make this part of our lives. I want us to go to Kenya next summer."

The seeds of our family Guatemala trip are planted with those words.

Of course, I'm excited to see my dad so happy. I'm also thrilled by the thought of Kenya and having a similar experience of feeling better about who I am.

❧❦

Feeling better will have to wait. Summer is filled with working and drinking and parties. There's also the routine arguments with dad… *You're not saving enough money … you're out too often and too late … you don't take your life seriously.* Each ends in the same predictable manner. I'm obstinate and he is obstinate until the frustration of it overwhelms me and I run to my room. We each go to our neutral corners to calm down. Then we manage through the conflict.

In these moments I grudgingly accept that I need to save more money. I also acutely feel his anxiety that college is near. It is getting closer to the day when I pack my belongings and move from the only home I've ever known. It's an anxiety I've felt since the day the letter arrived. There is no familiar model for me to follow and emulate. I'm the first and only member of my family to go through this experience.

Despite my outward confidence I'm fragile. The merry-go-round spins a little faster and there is only alcohol to slow it, to prop up my emotional fragility. So the drinking continues. The spinning slows and my anxiety and self-doubts are out of my head for a time.

I'm a different version of myself when drinking. I'm cool, social, outgoing, accepted, and supremely confident. *I'm going to kick college's ass* I think to myself as the warmth and security of alcohol flow through my body. It's a salve to my emotional dilemma: The deep desire to succeed at college versus the biting fear of loneliness and failure.

Unfortunately, its effects are only temporary. The worries continue without resolution.

❧❦

Before I know it, I'm packing for college. Zach is lying on my bed watching me. I move slowly, deciding what pieces of my high school self to bring to college. *So this is what it looks like to move out,* he seems to be thinking.

"I can't believe you're going," he says.

"Someday it'll be you."

"Yeah, not so long, I suppose."

"Where do you think you wanna go?"

"I don't know…some place that has baseball."

"I can see that."

"You nervous at all?"

"Nervous about what?"

"Leaving home, going to college."

"I don't know, not really," I lie.

I'm scared to be on my own. In my head I wonder, *Why would anyone want to know me? What is there to like about me? I've nothing to offer. Why do I think I can do this when I feel so scared and so small? What if I fail? It's entirely possible I'm going to fail. I don't know if I can do this…*

I try to project confidence, but my inner world is nothing more than my fears playing over and over inside my head. I'm inadequate, and my mind finds many small ways to remind me of this. I wish I could make it stop, but I can't. Inadequacy and uselessness is my internal monologue.

❦

The next morning mom is quiet, as dad and Zach put my things in the truck. She's done asking if I'm sure this is what I want. If I could have told her the truth, I would have said, *No, I'm not sure,* but I'm resigned to leaving. I'm standing in the doorway and I have to jump, but I'm not sure I'm wearing a parachute.

"It's not easy leaving," I say.

"I can't imagine it is," mom says.

"I don't know what it's going to be like."

"I don't either… Never been."

"It's hard to imagine what it's going to be like living on a dorm."

"Seems like a lot of kids without anyone to be responsible for 'em, if you ask me."

"Kids will be kids," I say smiling.

"Yeah, kids will be kids … That's kinda the point."

"Maybe we can move my things into the dorm and then I could stay with you and dad in the hotel tonight?"

"Yeah?"

"Yeah."

It's late summer, but I hear dad stomp his boots before coming in the house. Winter habits are hard to break.

"Ready?" he asks.

"I'm ready."

"Okay, let's go," he says slapping his hands together.

He walks very close and as we reach the truck he hugs me. His arms hold me tighter than he ever has before and I can feel it's hard to see me go. Then I climb in to the jump seat in the back next to Zach and the engine fires to life with a deep baritone throb. Our trip begins in silence.

In Duluth, we are met by my grandparents—mom's mom and dad—and my uncle Tony. Together we drop my things off in my dorm room and immediately leave to go to the hotel where they all have booked rooms. From there, we drove around Duluth sightseeing, which was mostly gaining different views of Lake Superior, and then ate out for dinner.

That night I sleep on a cot with mom and dad in the hotel. The next night I will be on my own in a dorm filled with kids and mom's words, *Kids will be kids*, echoes in my mind. I don't want to be a kid or for them to be kids. I'm hoping for mature and responsible, not the roughness of kids feeling the vulnerability of being on their own for the first time.

The next morning we eat breakfast. I'm nervous and probably talk too much, but I'm enjoying my family. Then we pile into our cars and drive to my dorm. Mostly, it's one uncomfortable hug after another. The exception is Zach who squeezes me harder than I think he ever has. I watch them pile into the cars, wave goodbye. In a few moments, despite being on a college campus filled with kids, I'm alone, truly, truly alone.

※※

I meet Jacob on the first day of college.

I'm walking through campus, lost, trying to find my Psychology class and can't make sense of the little map they gave us freshman at orientation. I look behind me and there is this guy following me. Not in a creepy way, but it feels uncomfortable.

"Are you looking for Psychology?" he asks.

"Yes. Are you?"

"I am, but I don't think we're anywhere near where we're supposed to be."

He looks around and asks someone who seems far more confident than the rest of us freshmen stumbling through campus like we are lost in the dark. The guy points to the building we were supposed to be in five minutes ago.

Jacob and I rush to class. It's hot and the sun is bright as we jog along. My backpack, filled with spanking new books and supplies, bounces against my body. Sweat droplets moisten the back of my t-shirt and I'm embarrassed to enter the room late and in this way.

"Can I sit next to you?" he asks as we slide into the room. The professor hasn't started speaking yet, so our entrance is a little less disruptive than I thought it would be.

"No problem my friends," the professor says in a full voice, like an actor on a stage, "I've gotten used to waiting for freshman to find their way here on the first day."

After class we walk together for a bit and talk. He asks where I'm from and I say Amery.

"I'm from a small town too," he says, "about 26,000 people."

"That's nothing. Amery's lucky if there're 3,000."

We part ways to make our next classes and I don't hear from him again for a couple of weeks. I meet a few people, but no one I really connect with. Life is mostly classes and homework and every now and again I go out with a few people or hang in someone's dorm room, but I'm not really drinking that much. The different, cool, social, version of me is largely dormant.

Running provides an opportunity to slow the merry-go-round and one day as I step out my dorm, Jacob sees me.

"Hey, you going for a run?" he asks.

"Yeah…"

"Mind if I join you?"

"Sure…"

As we jog, Jacob and I talk. There is something about him that feels familiar and easy. I still am my socially awkward self, but it doesn't matter so much with him. I don't see him as a potential boyfriend, just someone I can be friends with and that makes him a bit easier.

From that moment on, it's mostly just him and me hanging out as friends.

Our conversations quickly go from talking about college and our lives back home to more personal things. We share details about past loves, though there is little for me to tell, and we share our foibles and hidden stories. I tell him about my dad and what the experience of Vicki's death meant to my family. He listens attentively and talks about how he believes that God very likely meant for us to share that experience.

Jacob grew up in a family that fully embraces God and the Bible. They are open about their religion and faith and experience it with a sense of wonder and celebration. More than anyone I've ever met, he has a full understanding of his view on faith and the role that God plays in his life.

I believe mom and dad have a sense of faith, but we never go to church, nor does either of my parents or Zach openly discuss God. For both mom and dad, their childhoods and youth were defined by the strictness and emotional distance of their parents. For dad, agnosticism is a rebellion from and rejection of the authority of Mormonism in favor of a life devoid of organized religion, or really much thought on faith. For mom, agnosticism merely represents a shrug of the shoulders, *Who am I to know the nature or existence of God?*

However, I've always felt starved of faith, of a relationship with God. It is not that I seek religion so much as a consistent and fully defined sense of spirituality attached to a practice or expression of my faith, my personal beliefs in my higher power.

Seeing Jacob speak so openly and authoritatively about his faith, feeds that hunger and allows me to feel a closeness to him that is unique among any other friend I've ever had. It is an intimate friendship that does not cross the line from platonic to something deeper.

Our early conversations about God are mostly him explaining his point of view and beliefs. I listen to all he has to say, ask questions and share my own thoughts. As our friendship and emotional connection intensifies, we stay up late into the night and early morning hours talking.

One evening he asks if I would like to enjoy a couple cocktails and I agree. When I drink with Jacob it deepens, or perhaps exaggerates, the allure and my curiosity on matters of faith. After getting a little buzz, Jacob takes on a more charismatic and strong-minded approach to his faith and is more animated as he references passages from the Bible.

I'm absorbed, but I'm also acutely aware that I really have no relationship with God. I haven't experienced my higher power even as I've so strongly desired a connection with God. As our conversations progress, I'm almost jealous of how settled Jacob is in his faith and the relationship he seems to have with God.

It's now early November. Jacob and I are hanging out with friends. As usual there is beer or maybe some liquor, but we are absorbed in our own little world. He is talking of God again, describing the wonder of his relationship with God. His words stab at the God-sized hole I feel in my heart. It's a hole that I don't know how to fill or even if I can.

Jacob takes a breath and asks me if I'll go outside with him to smoke a cigarette.

The air is cold and bone-chillingly damp as we step outside. The leaves have long gone and a brisk wind skitters down the long finger that is the western end of Lake Superior. Jacob hunches his shoulders and holds one hand up to protect the flame from the lighter as he lights a cigarette. He then uncoils his body as he exhales. "Let's walk a little bit," he says.

We are silent as we walk up a small hill. Wet leaves line the sidewalk and the laughter of a couple girls echoes in the night.

"Do you know God?" Jacob asks me. "What is your relationship with God?"

"I don't know."

"I couldn't imagine that."

"Why?"

"The feeling of God in my life, of always having known God, is something that I can't imagine living without."

The strength of his faith and the confidence with which he speaks touches the emptiness in my heart. It is a sense of loneliness that I don't believe I've ever felt more deeply than in this moment. I wipe a tear from my eye.

"Why are you crying?" he asks.

"I've always been curious and wanted to know God, but I don't. I need to feel God in my life, to know him."

"Let me hold your hands."

I hesitate, "Jacob, I don't feel that way about you. You're just my friend."

"No, I know, just hold them."

I step toward him and grasp his outstretched hands as he closes his eyes. In an instant I feel a rush of adrenaline course through my body and my eyes are overwhelmed by whiteness. I'm in awe and overcome by the intensity and presence of this vision of flowing white light. I'm terrified, yet there is warmth and solace in this light. Is this God? Is this my higher power, my soul? What am I experiencing?

I pull my hands away, "What are you doing?!"

"I'm just praying."

My emotions wash over me like floodwaters breaching a dam and I begin to sob and laugh into my hands.

"What is it? What's wrong?" Jacob asks.

Looking up at him I ask, "What was that?"

"What was what?"

"The flowing light, the worm hole, the energy, am I imagining it?"

Jacob smiles, "That's the power and love of God I've been talking about. It is so huge, so immense…"

I turn from Jacob, "It was so beautiful."

"…even an infinitesimally small fragment of God…"

"Can it be real?"

"…is such powerful proof of your…"

"My relationship with God? Please let this be real."

It is a relationship founded on shaky ground. I have God in my life, but now I've to learn to live with God in my life. I'm filled with desire to be a woman of God, but I've yet to truly become the woman I'm meant to be.

※※

College is immense and I feel far from home. Though Jacob and I have formed a very tight friendship, I still struggle to create bonds with the people I meet. I'm envious of how easy it is for others to quickly form close friendships. I do spend time with a small group of friends, but the connection I feel for them is casual and lacks any true depth. I'm unable to open up to them and let them see my true self, which probably comes off as diffident or stuck up.

As the semester progresses, I'm more and more in the shadow of Jacob, the two of us lost in our own world as college life flows around us. I'm absorbed by his energy and feel unseen, like I'm invisible or eclipsed by his much brighter personality. I'm lonely for a broader social experience, but unsure how to reach out and grasp it.

My classes and course work are overwhelming as well. High school was relatively easy for me. Without much work, I was able to maintain A's and B's, but college is far more difficult. The material is more challenging and requires greater self-direction and discipline. I'm struggling to maintain a B and C average, which adds to my general sense of angst. I'm not failing, but I'm not succeeding to the degree that dad hopes.

Each morning I'm dogged by the thought that I may be letting my family down, that I can't handle college and shouldn't have tried. I need them and miss having them close by. I miss being able to sit in my car listening to tunes and talking with Zach about everything. I miss having dad so close, so encouraging even when it feels overbearing. And I miss my mom. I'm starved for affection.

I need to find that other version of myself. The one that is out-going and social; the one that can escape her problems and put the merry-go-round on hold for an evening. Like Popeye reaching for his can of spinach, I reach for a drink and then another and another. When I drink, I'm social and the challenges and setbacks of the day fade away.

Jacob drinks right along with me. By contrast, he becomes a proselytizer, a zealot, a missionary out to lecture and convert our college acquaintances to his way.

"Do you know God?" he asks the room. "I mean do you really know God and have you brought him and Jesus Christ into your life?"

"No Jacob," someone says, or, "Leave it alone Jacob."

"Well you should … you should. God is so amazing, so vast, so loving, so huge. How could you not have God in your life? How could you not reach out for God's love? I feel it right now and in every moment in my life."

"Enough Jacob," someone says.

"It's never enough. It could never be enough because Jesus Christ is my savior, he's your savior, and he brought God's love and light to this world. Come with me, reach out, hold yourself in the light and know God with me."

"Knock it off…"

"No, come on. Once you know Jesus, your life is going to be so much better than it is now…"

When sober, Jacob's charm and knowledge and love of God entice me. When drunk, his unyielding tirades and pugnacious evangelizing are annoying and difficult to take.

"Jacob, don't bring up God while I'm wasted right now," I say quietly to him after the bout of proselytizing passes.

"Is there ever a wrong time to share God's love, to bring Jesus into our lives?"

"Yeah, there is. We are drinking and not doing very good things and you're wasted, I'm wasted, so don't bring up God like that. Not now, not when we are doing things that are so far from God."

"But I've never felt closer to God than I do now. Every moment of my life I feel closer to God and if he is moving through me then so be it."

"Frankly, I don't want God to see me right now."

❦

When I start drinking I can't stop. I marvel at the people I drink with on a Tuesday night and they are up and at class Wednesday morning. I assume they drink like I do. Doesn't everybody? So if I'm in such pain, how can they manage even a pale appearance at some morning class when I cannot?

When I'm drinking, I do not make good decisions. My thinking is not clear and life slips. It happens slowly at first, but there is an unyielding momentum to it. I cross the line with Jacob and our relationship becomes physical, even though I know I'm not and never really have been physically attracted to him.

When I'm drinking, I may slow the merry-go-round for an evening, but it spins all that much faster the next day. I'm falling behind in school, I'm lonelier than I've ever been, and I'm allowing my emotions to be manipulated by Jacob, but I don't know what to do. I'm lost and I drink so these hard things fade away.

When I'm drinking, I feel as if I'm a passenger in my own life. I want to love God, I want meaningful friendships, and I want to do well in school, but alcohol, insecurity and anxiety impel me down a much different path.

❦

I go home for Thanksgiving, but there is no way I'm going to share with mom and dad how I'm doing in school or that I'm unhappy. I put on a happy face and say things such as, *My professors are all so interesting. You should meet my Psyche professor, he is one of the most intense people I've ever known. College is much harder than high school, but I'm working hard and doing pretty well. My friends are from all over the place and there is this one girl who is sooooo funny... and yeah, there is a boy I kinda like...*

All of it is lies and half-truths to sate mom and dad's curiosity. I'm a huckster selling a story of a college stereotype to two unwitting marks. I'm ashamed and think to myself, *I do not want God to see me right now.*

With each of my stories Zach presses his lips together and his eyes are dark and piercing.

"Why are you saying these things to mom and dad?" he asks the night before I have to go back to Duluth as we sit in my car listening to music. "You're lying. I know you're lying."

"I'm not lying about everything."

"No?"

"No, I'm not." I turn my head to look him directly in the eye, "So, how are you doing in school?"

"Not well."

"Yeah?"

"Yeah… and that's the truth."

I turn the music up and the two of us look out into the starless night.

❧❧

The night I come back to school, Jacob walks into my dorm room. My roommate looks up at him, marks the page in the textbook she'd been reading and leaves the room.

"I've something for you."

I look at him, but feel nothing. He hands me a book in a brown paper wrapping. I peel the wrapping off and it's a Bible.

"I told my mom about you and she wanted you to have this." He pulls the Bible from my hands and sits down on my bed. I sit next to him and he leafs through the pages to the New Testament and begins to read his favorite passages.

"It feels good to have God in your life, doesn't it?" he asks.

"Yeah, it does. I'm very glad for this relationship." His eyes brighten. "I mean with God."

Thanksgiving offered a break from the routine I've fallen into, but it begins apace once I'm back at school. Jacob is always present and always talking about God. I'm interested and intrigued as I explore my relationship with God through Jacob, but continue to wonder why I have such a strong compulsion to be with him. Other than drinking and God, there is no basis for our relationship, but I can't break away from him.

Mercifully, I glide through the next few weeks after Thanksgiving without causing any further damage to my grades even as my drinking and depression mount. By the day of my last final for the fall semester I feel uneasy as I wait for mom and dad to pick me up for Christmas break. I miss them, but I know I haven't done well in my school work. Certainly nothing they'd be proud of; probably more concerned. Even still, I can't wait to be out of this dorm, out of Duluth and back home.

❧※❦

It's good to be home, but the lies persist. Though my grades did not fall through the floor, they're not that great either.

"When do we see the grades?" my dad asks.

"I don't know. I don't know when I can check them online."

"How do you think you did?"

"Pretty good, probably A's and B's."

Then there are the lies about my life at school.

"How are all of those friends doing? Gosh, I don't think I can remember their names, but you know who I mean," mom says.

"Their doing really awesome... I miss them so much."

"And the boy?"

"He's great mom, but it's nothing. We're just good friends"

The only moments of honesty are in my car, listening to music with Zach.

"I don't like school," I tell him.

"What do you mean?"

Tears well in my eyes, "I'm not happy there and I'm not doing well."

"Why?"

"Because I'm partying too much and spending way too much time with this guy," I sob.

Zach looks at me. His eyes soften, "What's up with the guy?"

"I don't know. He and I spend all of our time together and drink pretty much every night, so I know he isn't any good for me, but at the same time there's something about him I can't quite let go of."

"Is he why you're partying so much?"

"No. I don't need his help doing that."

"Yeah, I know."

"But I feel so lonely Zach, like I miss you and mom and dad all the time even though mom and dad are so hard to deal with."

"I'd miss them too."

"I feel like I don't have anyone to talk to, who knows me and who I can really talk with, ya know? Like, well, now, sitting here with you. It just sucks, but when I drink or when I'm with Jacob it doesn't feel so bad even though I know I probably shouldn't be doing those things and it feels like that's all I do now when I'm at school."

"Maybe you should come home."

"What?"

"Get your stuff and come home."

"I don't know Zach. That feels like giving up. Dad would kill me."

"Not if you tell him what's going on."

"I don't know."

"You can always go back, right?"

"I don't know." Outside the world is white and cold. There is a thick belt of stars through the tree branches. Zach and I are quiet and in my head I pray to God, *Please make next semester better than this one. Please help me find my way so I'm not so lonely.*

"Zach, have you thought about God?"

Zach scratches at an imaginary spec on the window next to him, "No, not really."

"Do you believe in God?"

"I think so, but I don't really know."

"I do. God came into my life this past semester."

"You mean you converted to a religion?"

"No. I've always wanted to have a relationship with God, to know what he or it is and to feel it in my life."

"Oh. How'd that happen?"

"Jacob has been helping me understand the Bible better and sharing with me the role that God plays in his life."

"I don't know Sarah, he doesn't seem like he's all that healthy for you."

"God?" I say smiling at Zach.

He folds his arms and turns away from me to look out the window, "No, Jacob."

"Maybe… Do you wanna go to church with me tomorrow?"

"No, I don't think so."

⁂

Dad doesn't ask me about my grades for the remainder of Thanksgiving break. I suppose he still trusts that I wouldn't lie to him about that. And then, all too soon, I'm back in my dorm room unpacking my bag. My roommate is either not back yet or out and I'm alone.

My movements are slow and I just throw my clothes into drawers without really thinking about it. Since my parents left, my eyes have been moist and I feel as if I'm on the verge of letting go and sobbing into my pillow. *I don't know what I'm doing here… I can't handle this… I just want to go home… I just want to go home.*

There's a knock at the door. I wipe my eyes and say come in. I turn and there is Jacob.

"Hey, some friends have a bunch of beer, let's go," he says.

I look at him, but I don't feel anything other than relief that I'm not alone. "Yeah, okay, that sounds good." I toss my bag in the corner and the two of us go and get drunk. The next day I skip my 8 am Microbiology class.

As the semester wears on, Jacob and I drink more and more. Whether it's a bottle of rum or a case of beer, we plow through them and I'm thirsty for more. Each night I know that if I drink I'll miss my morning class and probably the others as well.

There is a constant battle between the guilt of not doing well in school and the overwhelming desire to drink. More often than not I choose alcohol rather than labor with loneliness and depression. It is too easy to slide into the other version of myself and let her take over for the evening. She is confident, happy and social. The version of me that is lonely, scared and overflowing with anxiety is tucked safely away and watches from a distance.

The morning comes and I'm back in possession of my horribly hung-over mind and body.

❖❖❖

After Easter break, Jacob and I are inseparable. We feed off each other's companionship. He is like a satellite, always in orbit around me, but I maintain an emotional distance from him. We are close, but in the back of my mind is the nearly constant thought that this boy is unhealthy, that this boy will not become the man I spend my life with. But I cannot and will not break free of him. He is the sop for my loneliness and I believe he is a connection to God.

The mysterious power of alcohol is that it enables denial, delusion and grandiosity even as it is self-evident that life is spiraling out of control. It is the catalyst of hypocrisy by cleaving truth from the concept of self for as long as its effects are felt. The next morning truth comes rushing in with the pain of the hang-over.

I start smoking. I gain 30 pounds. I stop dressing myself and spend most days in sweats and slippers. April comes and I'm drinking every day, sometimes starting in the afternoon and going into the morning hours. I've long since given up on my 8 am Microbiology class. My noon Psychology class falls by the wayside as well. The lonely, scared and depressed me is humiliated and filled with guilt.

The alternative version of me doesn't care.

One night I'm drinking wine with a friend of Jacob's in an on-campus apartment for older students. I don't care about anything. I just want to get drunk, to have fun. It's a relatively short walk to my dorm, but I'm so drunk that I let myself pass out on a couch next to Jacob.

In the middle of the night my eyes open to one of the men living in the apartment on top of me. His hair is long and tangled and his face is covered by a dark, shaggy beard. He's pulled my pants down and stares silently at me.

I push up on his chest, but my arms feel weak, "What are you doing? Get off of me!"

He climbs off and runs down the hall to his bedroom.

I pull my pants up, but I'm still very drunk and I fall back to sleep. I don't know how much time passes, but I wake up to this man pulling my pants down again.

"Get away from me!" He runs off down the hallway to his room and I pull my pants up and fall asleep.

I wake up a third time to this man trying to take my pants off. I yell at him and he runs down the hall again.

"Jacob, Jacob…. get up… we have to leave. Now!"

The next day I don't say anything to the school. I don't say anything to anyone. I just don't care anymore. I'll drink tonight and last night will simply fade away.

❈ ❈

Zach is an amazingly intuitive person.

I talk with him more than my dad. Even though I'm relatively honest with Zach, I still can't bring myself to tell him everything. I can't tell him how much I'm drinking or that I've essentially given up on school.

The day after the weirdo pulled my pants down, I wake up at four in the afternoon to my cell phone.

Zach hears sleep dripping from my mouth as I say hello.

"Sarah, are you still in bed?"

I don't even have the energy to come up with a plausible excuse so I tell him, "I'm really hung over Zach."

"What are you doing?"

"Zach, please don't tell mom or dad that I'm still in bed."

This isn't the first clue I've given as to what my life has become.

A few weeks earlier, Easter Sunday, the one-year anniversary of my first drink, I was riding in the back of mom's car on our way to our grandparents'. A burst of wind blew the car and I leaned my face against the window glass and looked up. The sky was striated by bands of slate grey clouds whose shadows moved quickly across the earth. Sunlight shown down through cloud breaks like frosted beams of light.

In the sky high above our car a lone raven bounced and wobbled on drafts of wind. I felt that I was being blown by unfriendly winds and felt terribly alone even though I was surrounded by my family. There was so much I wanted to tell them, needed to tell them, but I couldn't.

"Sarah," Zach whispered, "why are you crying?"

"I don't know."

"What's wrong with you?"

"Nothing."

"Sarah, there's something wrong."

I was lonely and depressed, but all I said was, "I don't know."

It isn't hard for Zach to connect the car trip over Easter to me being in bed and hung over at four in the afternoon.

"Zach did you hear me? Please don't tell mom and dad I'm in bed this late."

"Sarah, you never drank this much before meeting Jacob."

"I know."

"If you're going to be with somebody, you should be happy, but you're really depressed. He's not right for you."

"I know Zach, I know…"

"Come home Sarah, please?"

"I can't. I have to try and make this work."

"You shouldn't be with him… you're miserable."

"I know."

I feel sick after I hang up the phone. I know I can't pull my life together and miraculously find my bearings.

About a half-hour later dad calls.

"Sarah, what's going on? You're sleeping at four in the afternoon?"

"Dad, it's my first time drinking and I don't know how to handle it, okay?"

"I don't know, Sarah."

"Dad, I didn't have that much at all"—I drank an entire box of wine—"and it really hit me because I'm not used to it. I swear, everything is okay… lesson learned… alright?"

Dad paused for a moment. "We'll see. So it looks like Kenya isn't going to work."

Ugh, the one thing I'd been looking forward to. "What do you mean?"

"There's been violence there around their elections so it isn't going to work out for us."

"I'm sorry… that's too bad."

"It doesn't mean we can't go on a trip, though. There's a group going to a small village in Guatemala in August. Whatta ya think of that?"

"Sounds good dad. I don't know all that much about Guatemala, but I can't wait."

"Neither can I."

I hear his smile through his voice. He's proud and I know how hard he's worked to make this happen. For most of the winter he's worked three or more jobs. He's a good man and I miss him. I also know that as he's gotten up at 5 am every day and worked into the night to make this trip happen for our family, I've been drinking college away.

I feel panicked and I don't know what to do.

"I love you dad."

"Love you too. Be good, my love."

That night I go out and get drunk again.

❧❧

Finally, thankfully, mercifully, I wake up to the pain of another hang over and surrender. I've had enough. My body, my soul, my heart feel agonizingly, achingly hollow. I realize that I need to go home. I can't bear the weight of my loneliness and depression any longer. Even the thought of admitting to dad that I've failed feels less horrible than what it would take to endure one more minute of this life.

"Mom, I really need to come home."

"Okay honey, if this is what you need to do we'll come and get you."

She doesn't ask why. She doesn't judge. She doesn't make me feel any worse than I already do. She is my mom and she loves me unconditionally. I know the conversations will come, but for now, I need mom and dad and Zach.

I pull my body out of bed and call Jacob.

"I'm going home," I tell him.

"What?"

"I'm going home. I can't be here anymore."

"What about us? What does this mean?"

"I don't know. All I know is that I have to leave." The truth is I don't care about leaving Jacob or anything other than going home and feeling better. *To heck with all of it,* I thought, *I've already failed all of my classes. It just doesn't matter anymore.*

Mom arrives early in the afternoon. I'm wearing a sweatshirt, pajama pants and slippers. I still feel sick from the night before and I'm exhausted.

"Look at you," she says.

I feel my cheeks burn, "I know… not quite the pretty girl I used to be."

"She's still in there." Mom looks at the few bags I've packed. "Is this it?"

"Yeah." I don't tell her that I'm just leaving the rest of my stuff. I'll get it another time.

"Alright," she sighs.

It takes just a couple of trips to load my stuff in the car. I don't know where my roommate is. No need to say goodbye to her. I never really knew her and she probably hates me anyway.

I get in the car and lean my head against the window.

"I'm sorry, mom."

"It's okay honey. We'll figure it out."

"Is dad mad?"

"He's not really mad… worried about you more than anything."

"Mom," my eyes well and my voice shakes, "I'm really, really depressed."

Mom sets her eyes forward and wheels the car away from the dorm, "I know honey. We're going to help you."

I wipe my eyes with the sleeve of my sweatshirt. "Dad says we're going to Guatemala."

"Yep… Kenya isn't gonna work out."

I remember dad coming home from Kenya, "I think that's gonna be good for me."

"I think it's gonna be good for all of us. I just hate the flying part," she says smiling at me.

"It'll be okay."

"I know." Mom taps the gas pedal and we lurch into traffic. I close my eyes and feel the school and then Duluth getting further away. *I'm done...no more...no more,* I think to myself as I fade into sleep.

Chapter 8

Falling

When mom brings me home I intend to start listening to my higher power; to live my life closer to God's love for me; and to leave Jacob for good and give up drinking.

I want to make dad proud again.

Mom and dad do their best to help me. Dad wants me to deal with my depression so he takes me to a doctor who prescribes antidepressants and therapy. I do the pills, but not the therapist.

Then he takes me to a drug and alcohol counselor to be assessed for alcoholism. Dad is in the room as I answered the questions, so I don't feel very comfortable. I shade the truth about how much I drink. Even still, the counselor diagnoses me with alcoholism.

"You know, Sarah" he says, "Alcoholism's a progressive disease and if you continue to drink, it'll only get worse."

"It will," echoes dad. He leans forward, eyes wide and hands clasped in his lap. "I started with just a few puffs of meth, but it nearly killed me and almost landed me in jail."

"You *were* arrested," I remind him.

"Sarah," the counselor says leaning in, "alcohol is also a depressant. Do you know what that means?"

"No."

"It means that if you stop drinking now, you could probably stop taking those pills pretty soon."

I'm not angry at either of them. I understand what they both are saying and I see dad's worry in his eyes, but I don't want to be told what to do. I can control what I do, who I am.

I want the love of both God and my family, but I set conditions and place terms on both. On some level, I'm in a state of personal and spiritual denial. It should be easy to open my heart to their love, but I can't.

❧

Two weeks pass and I start feeling better and I miss Jacob.

"Stay with us," dad pleads.

I feel better and I'm bored and want to be on my own again. The thought of summer spent working the same waitressing job with the same Amery people is more than I can bear. I pack my stuff in my car and move back to Duluth. My plan is to waitress, save money for Guatemala, and go back to college after the trip.

In Duluth I work, share a cramped apartment with two other roommates, drink, and fall back with Jacob. The voices of God and my family are never far from my mind or heart, but alcohol, immaturity and insecurity are nearly enough to drown them out.

I'm not happy, again.

Then one day Jacob comes to me while I'm doing a couple dishes in the kitchen of my apartment, "I slept with someone." He just stands there with his arms folded, leaning against the counter by the sink. There's a churlish look to his eyes. He's thrown down a challenge, now he's waiting to see what happens next, like it's more a curiosity, a test, *What will she do?*

"What do you mean?"

"I have to be honest with you. I slept with someone else."

I smack him across his face and run off.

I don't know what to do. I don't want to go home because I'm embarrassed for my family to know this about me, but I need them. I need Zach. I need to sit with him in my car listening to music again. I need to hear his voice, even though I know he will be honest to the point it will pain me.

I start driving home when my phone rings. It's Zach.

"What the heck is going on?" he asks. "Jacob just told me he cheated on you."

"It's true," I sob, "I'm lost and I don't know what to do."

The decision of whether to tell my parents is no longer mine. Zach tells mom and dad. Dad calls right away.

"Get home now."

When I pull into the driveway, dad comes straight out of the house and hugs me. I know Zach and mom are inside watching.

Then he holds me at arm's length and looks straight into my eyes, "Once a cheater always a cheater. This guy's no good and he's got to go."

I fall into his arms sobbing, "I know, I know, I know…"

But I still am not done. I haven't yet given in to my higher power. I still believe I can fight all my battles on my own and set conditions on how I do that.

I haven't forgiven Jacob, but I go back to Duluth with dad's last words reverberating in my head, "He's no good for you, stay here with us."

It's August and there are only two weeks until we leave for Guatemala. My plan is to keep working (I needed the money), go to Guatemala, get my head together helping build a school for people whose lives are worse than my own, and then go to community college in Amery.

Like dad, Guatemala is a chance at redemption.

But Guatemala isn't for a few weeks. I don't have to start being the person I plan to be yet. I keep drinking and fall further into depression. As the saying goes, *My slip is showing.* Conversations with dad don't go well. I talk to Zach and rather than keep what I say to himself, he shares it with mom and dad.

"Sarah isn't doing well," he tells dad after hanging up the phone with me.

"I know," he says. "Zach, I think it's time to go get her and bring her home."

I have never seen dad allow anyone to drive his truck, but he hands Zach the keys. Dad's already called to tell me Zach is coming to get me. No discussion. This is how it's going to be.

❧ ❧

"Do you want to drink?" I say holding a bottle of gin toward Zach soon after he arrives at my small Duluth apartment.

"No, Sarah I don't."

"Okay," I say, "Suit yourself."

He falls asleep early. I drink the gin by myself.

Zach wakes me the next morning, but I'm too hung over to get up. I tell him to leave in the truck. I'll drive my car later.

Later, I drive my car down to the house. We're leaving for Guatemala the next day, but I feel horrible. I pray, *God, please give me the strength to heal myself.*

Dad comes out of the house and hugs me.

"I love you very much Sarah, but you're home now, to stay," he says.

"I know dad. Guatemala and home."

"Get your old job, save some money, go to community college."

"Okay."

"You need a degree to make it in this world and I want you to have that, okay?"

As he says these words, in my mind I am already putting conditions on what I'm willing to do, how far I'm willing to follow *his* plan, or for that matter, *His* plan.

Two days later, dad and Zach are dead. Two weeks after that, I go home for the first time. I feel God's hand working within my life, but I haven't yet truly found his presence within me.

⋙ ⋘

It's twilight as I pull into our driveway. The woods are thick and alive with a gentle passing breeze. There is a sense of escape as the Jeep approaches the house. The world is being held at bay by a wall of green. To the west, the horizon is saturated by a deep Parrish blue that ebbs into an inky blackness, accentuated by emerging starlight.

This is the first time I've been to the house since the crash. The last two weeks have been a blur of drinking, caring for mom as much as I can, tending to the business of death, and staying with friends in Minneapolis, as near to mom as possible.

I'm alone and it feels hard to see my family's home, knowing that dad and Zach will never be here again. Off to one side of the driveway is dad's green Ford F150. Seeing it looking just as dad left it, so clean and obsessively well cared for, reminds me of how unusual it was for him to have sent Zach in it to pick me up in Duluth. He must have been so worried, so anxious to have me home. I don't think even mom was allowed to drive it, just Zach, that one day.

I'm in mom's Jeep, which is the car we all rode to the airport in. Dad driving, mom sitting nervously in the passenger seat, Zach and me in the back, ear-buds jammed in our ears, zoning out to music. The day before Zach unpacked my stuff from the truck and left it in my room. Later, I came home hung over to a mess of boxes and clutter laid haphazardly around my room.

"When we get back from Guatemala, I'll help you unpack and set your room up again," he said.

Earlier today, I spent more than two hours driving around the mass of parking areas at Minneapolis-St. Paul International Airport looking for the jeep with Becky, my half-sister. For the life of me I couldn't remember where we'd parked the day we caught the plane. I only remember Zach typing the location in his cell phone. It never occurred to me to pay attention to where we parked or that I'd need to know where.

"Are you sure you don't remember where you all parked?" asked Becky for the hundredth time. The parking lot was huge and each aisle looked exactly like every other. Every so often we'd see a Jeep or car that looked like it, only to have our hopes dashed as we neared it.

"No, I don't, can you stop asking?" Becky patted my leg. "I'm only 19, why do I have to have this all on me?"

Becky's mouth flattened. "You're not the only one who lost a father."

"I'm sorry. Sometimes I forget he was your dad too." I looked out into the shimmering heat of the asphalt parking lot. My mouth tasted like stomach acid and my head pounded from drinking the night before.

"Is that it?" Becky asked pointing toward the end of the aisle.

I sat up for a moment, "No, I don't think so."

❦❦

Eventually, we found the Jeep. I hugged Becky goodbye and told her I'll probably see her the next day at the hospital. As I unlocked and opened the Jeep's door, I expected to hear dad say, "Not today girl, dad's drivin'."

Opening the door was like opening a time capsule to when my family was whole and alive. The car was clean, as usual, but there were small pieces here and there of dad and Zach and mom. I could still feel the pressure of their bodies on the seats and smell the feint residue of dad's cigarettes. Zach had left a ball cap in the back. I picked it up and sniffed the brim hoping for a wisp of his scent.

I climbed in, shut the door, started the engine, cranked the AC, and pressed my face into my hands sobbing. It was the first time I cried since the crash.

For two weeks now, I've felt nothing.

"What are you doing?" my friend Kayla asked when she first saw me only a couple days after the crash. I was drunk, very drunk. Smiling and laughing.

"I'm fine, it's okay."

"Really?" Kayla asked.

"Yeah, everything's going to be okay," I lied. I love Kayla, but she doesn't have anything to offer that I need.

"Are you sure?" her eyes pinched together and her head tilted. "I mean…. You saw Zach and your dad die, didn't you?"

Kayla's eyes widened; then she looked down to the drink in my hand, "I'm sorry, is that insensitive of me?"

I shift my weight sideways, "No, everyone wants to know what happened."

In the Jeep, emotions came in torrents. Sadness, depression, feeling sorry for myself…. Pain. *How could this be happening? Zach and dad are dead and mom is really, really hurt… I'm so alone.*

It all felt so surreal. Until that moment, I was surrounded by people; grandma and grandpa Jensen, grandma and grandpa Spike, Becky, Uncle Myron and Uncle Scott; then drinking with friends as soon as I can get away from my family and the hospital.

Sitting in mom's Jeep was the first moment I've had alone. I try and process all of it…. The crash, the ride through the jungle to the hospital in Zacapa then on to Guatemala City. The flight home floating through the clouds. The effort of trying to get Zach and dad's bodies home.

In the back of my mind throughout these two weeks are the words of the male nurse in Guatemala City, *Your life was spared for a reason. You have a lot to accomplish in this world.*

A few days after the crash, I wrote in my journal, *I guess I'm not sure what I'm thinking or feeling, but I do know I'm so thankful to still be alive. I also know that I have a purpose on this beautiful earth. I want to help people, change people's lives, and I feel I have the ability to do so.*

Thinking about these words now, I don't know why I wrote this. How can I help anyone when I can't seem to even help myself? But I do know that this is what I want for my life. I don't know how to get there.

After two weeks of drinking, caring for mom, and dealing with the business of death, I have no idea how I am ever going to be that person, the person I am supposed to become.

※※

I park the Jeep next to dad's truck and sit for a moment after turning the engine off.

In front of me is the gas-powered machine dad used to mill his own lumber from trees on our property. There are fresh-cut boards neatly stacked around his modest sawmill. A layer of greying wood chips coats the ground. Felled timber is stacked like pickup sticks only a few feet away.

He was the 9-to-5 man's version of a weekend lumberjack.

I step out of the Jeep and climb the porch steps. We are (or should I now say *were*) a family of loners. No one comes to feed the cats or tend to the house. Cat food is left on the porch in a big dispenser contraption dad rigged up. It's nearly empty and Blackie and Snowball wander up to me, meowing, excited in that calculated cat way. I reach down and pet them; feel their coarse fur in my hands. Then I walk into the kitchen. It's as clean as we left it.

Blackie and Snowball follow me in, casual and cool, as if the world is perfectly okay. They meow and rub against my leg, happy to see me. I put some food in their bowls.

In the living room the smell of pine is comforting; its home.

I sit on the couch and the cats come in and crawl up around me. Blackie curls up on my lap and immediately begins to purr. Snowball lays his long body along my thigh and licks her paws.

I'm home, but it's too quiet. Zach's dirty cereal bowl and glass aren't left on the side table. Mom isn't puttering in the kitchen. Music isn't thrumming from Zach's room. Looking out the front window, I see dad's woodshop is silent and dark.

I have never experienced loneliness like this. I thought I knew sadness, emotional pain, hopelessness, but this is something completely different, more intense, deeper. My entire body is in pain. My head and heart feel as if they're on fire. I keep reaching for my cell phone to call out for help, but Zach is dead. Dad is dead.

My mind won't stop. Their bodies, mom's screams. *Don't leave me Sarah, please God, don't leave me Sarah....* Dad's foot and leg jutting out from under the plane wreckage, the explosion, mom's blackened flesh. All of it loops continually in my mind. *I...can't...shut...it...off.*

"There must be something to drink. Mom wouldn't let us run out of Bud light."

In the refrigerator there is nearly a full twelve-pack of beer. I grab one and pop it open. The first sip is reassuring, but it's not enough. Alcohol is no longer about becoming the other Sarah, but trying to medicate pain.

I take another sip and walk into the living room, up the stairs and into mom and dad's room, what we called the loft. The bed is made, but dad's clothes are still piled on their couch. *Geez dad, you've got a lot of clothes, but you always wear the same thing.*

I pick up a shirt and dad's scent is still on it. I close my eyes and I see him. Gone is the dishonest meth addict; replaced by a man who is strong and honest. A hard worker who is passionate about everything he does and doesn't half-ass anything. He is a real, true man.

*I love you Sarah, but you need a degree to make it in this world and I want you to have that. H*is words, straight-forward and honest, come to me. My eyes well up with tears and I remember my dorm room in Duluth, the throbbing head and acidic stomach of a hangover, overcast sky, being lost… and then the look in dad's eyes when I stepped out of mom's car.

I was pale, fatter than I'd ever been, my eyes dark. *Sarah, its okay… we'll get you through this.* But I knew it wasn't okay. I wanted to lean into him, to be held by him and just let my body and mind go; to vanish into his strong arms, but I couldn't. It's only now that he's gone that I truly feel that I could accept what he had to offer, that I need him.

"I love you Sarah," he said.

"I love you too."

The look in his eyes won't leave me; the disappointment they so clearly expressed. My shoulders shake, as spasms of tears and sorrow and regret carom through my body.

I fold the shirt under my arm and sip more beer. The bottle is nearly empty, so I go to the kitchen and grab another.

I don't want to go to my room. Zach's room is off the kitchen where mom and dad could see in, so he kept it clean. Everything is right where he left it. I take a long pull of the beer bottle. I want more, I feel like I need more, but I'm too tired and feeling pretty buzzed, anyway.

I crawl into Zach's bed, still wearing my t-shirt and shorts. The air is warm. My cheeks are salty from tears.

The cats leap onto the bed and curl themselves at my feet. I click the light off and tuck dad's shirt next to my body. Staring up at the ceiling, I think of God and pray, *Please help me. I want to be in your warmth, closer to you, your child. I miss Zach so much. I miss us staying up late talking, talking about girls, boys, life, God. He was my best friend. What am I going to do? Please God, give me strength and help me not to worry about things that I have no control over. I need you to help me through this.*

As I pray, I'm reminded of the last time Zach and I spoke in his room. It was the night before leaving for Guatemala. "I believe there's a power in the universe that is so much bigger than us, that created everything."

"I don't know Sarah. I'm not sure about the idea of some gray-haired guy watching over us."

"I know, but that's not really what God is to me. When I think of the word God, I picture a man with a thick, dramatic-looking white beard. That's what the Bible says, but it feels too immense; like *God* is everybody's and it doesn't signify my connection. That God is too generic or something."

Zach looks away, "I don't know."

I tried again. "I suppose God is the proper term, but I think of it as my higher power because it's mine. It's my relationship. It's my connection. It's special. No one can tell me anything about my relationship with God because it's mine, it's *my* higher power. Nobody else knows about this relationship, but me and God.

"I guess, I don't believe it's possible to sum up God because it's something too vast, too unknowable. I read the Bible, but really its one small view into something that's huge, that spans the universe. My higher power is my small slice of that. It's that bit of whatever God is that's for me, that watches over me, that I can communicate with and pray to."

"I suppose that's what I would believe too."

"You have a higher power. You just have to open your eyes to it."

"Maybe." Zach cracked his knuckles and the corners of his mouth curled underneath the peach fuzz coating his upper lip. "But I do know that on my death bed I'll be praying to Jesus."

Remembering his grin makes me smile as I lie in Zach's bed. *I want to live for you, God; I want my life to mean something. I want to be your child, a child of God. I can't wait to be Sarah Jensen, the person I'm supposed to be. I just need to find the strength.*

I don't know who it is I'm supposed to be, but I know I have to change. I can't change that dad and Zach are dead and mom is essentially lost to me, but if I'm going to survive this I have to change. So many of my choices have only made me miserable, and now its misery piled upon misery.

❧※❧

The next day I'm in the foyer of a funeral home in Isanti, Minnesota, with Grandmother and Grandfather Jensen (dad's parents), and the funeral director. We're making arrangements for the funeral, flowers for the tops of the caskets, food, that sort of thing. It's taken these past two weeks for their bodies to finally return from Guatemala.

"Mom asked if they could be buried next to Aunt Vicki," I tell them.

Grandmother rubs the corner of one eye, "Okay." Grandfather looks down at his feet and says nothing.

I want to wait to bury Zach and dad so mom could be there, but the funeral director tells me we can't. They have to be buried soon, unless we want their bodies cremated.

"No, we don't want that," I tell him. He's an older man, dark suit, polite, and soft eyes.

"Okay," he says. "Your father and brother are downstairs if you would like to see the caskets."

"Can I see the bodies?" The funeral director looks at Grandfather.

"I don't think you want to do that Sarah," Grandfather says.

Even though I know their bodies are burned beyond recognition, that they have been dead for two weeks, I can't help but ask to see them, to know fully that they are gone. "The last I saw of either of them was dad's leg," I say. "I think I want to see their bodies."

The funeral director's eyes widen, "I'm sorry, but we can't do that. The caskets have already been sealed."

We walk downstairs to the funeral home's basement to a softly decorated room where the caskets are on display. Both caskets are silver with rails running down the side so they can be carried. Zach's casket is the smaller of the two. I just stare at them and begin to cry. Grandmother puts her hand to her chin and Grandfather stands with his hands held behind his back. Both are as quiet as Stoics.

"Here," says the funeral director handing me a small, square box of tissues. After a few moments he says, "We'll need to select a liner that each casket will be sealed in once they are in the ground."

I barely hear or acknowledge him.

"Would you like to see the choices we offer?"

"I don't know," I say without looking at him.

"I'll take care of this, Sarah," Grandfather says and he walks off with the funeral director.

"I think I want to see them go into the ground so I can get some closure on all of this," I say to Grandmother.

She sniffles, "Me too."

※※

In the afternoon I walk into mom's room in the burn unit at Hennepin County Health Center. Becky is there as well as Grandma and Grandpa Spike.

Mom can't move. There are tubes running into her nose, an IV line poking into the top of her hand, heart monitor lines spider out from beneath her Johnny. She has a colostomy because everything below her stomach is so badly burned, and a catheter tube emerging from the foot of her bed and into a bag held by a hook at the bottom of her bed. Her lips are blistered and chapped and a ventilator tube emerges from her mouth to help her breath.

She's been in an induced coma for the past 20 hours. The doctors are removing strips of skin from her back to use as grafts for her legs, which would be overwhelmingly painful if she were awake. Each of these surgeries, there will be many, require her to be in a medical coma for 24 hours. This is her second. After the last, when she woke up, the pain was almost unendurable.

She looks so helpless, not the strong woman tending to her gardens and relentlessly mowing the yard. The image of dad and Zach's coffins passes through my mind. *This is what my family has come to,* I whisper to myself.

"It hurts to see her like this," I say to no one in particular. "I don't know what I'd ever do without her."

"She's a fighter," Becky says.

"I know." I remember her screams as she was trapped in the burning plane. "Have the doctors said anything? Will they be waking her up soon?"

"Soon, I think," Becky says. She glances at Grandma and Grandpa Spike then back to me. "How are you?"

"I just want all of this to be over."

In my head I'm screaming to get out of here, to my friend's apartment, and drink. I want to put all of this out of my mind. I want off the merry-go-round for just a little bit, to stop feeling everything so intensely.

"I'll be back in a minute," I say as I walk into the hallway.

"Sarah?" asks a voice behind me. I turn and it's one of mom's doctors. "How are you?"

"I'm fine. How's mom?"

"She's stable."

"I just want this all to be over." I feel like a broken record.

"I'm sorry, but your mom is going to have to be here for a while."

"What? A month, two months?"

The doctor's lips flatten, "Probably around five or six depending on how the grafts go."

"Five or six?" I can't believe what I've just heard. It's a constant drip, drip, drip of stuff going wrong. "What am I going to do? Where am I going to live? I'm only 19. I just want my mom back!"

"I know."

I cover my face with my hands then look at the doctor, "I don't know how to be strong anymore, but everyone wants me to be strong, they expect it from me, but I just can't do it anymore."

"Have you spoken with a therapist?"

"Who?"

"A therapist to help you sort through all of this… emotionally."

"No."

"Hasn't anyone said anything to you; offered any help, emotionally?"

"It's not really my family's way." I think of dad and how he quit meth on his own. No help.

He folds his arms across his body, "You need help and I think you should see a therapist. We have a social worker here that I think can help you find someone good."

My spine stiffens at being told what to do, "I've never been to a therapist."

"We'll find you one and you go."

I roll my eyes, *One more thing I have to do.* Down the hall, past the doctor, there's a man being wheeled from his room in a bed. A female nurse leans over the nurse's station desk to grab a pen.

"I don't know," I say.

"Do it."

Chapter 9

Finding Pauline

Sarah?"

"Yes…"

"Please," she says holding her office door open, "come in."
I walk past her feeling as if she is studying me.

"Why don't you take the larger chair," she says gesturing toward a peach-colored couch with a few decorative pillows. She sits down into black, wooden chair with leather seat and back. "I'm Dr. Pauline Boss, but I suppose you already know that."

Looking at her for the first time, Dr. Boss is almost exactly how I imagined her. She's probably in her late 50s, graying blond hair. She's wearing a green blouse underneath a loose, black V-neck sweater, and black slacks. Glasses with thick, black frames sit tightly on the bridge of her nose. A strand of turquois beads spills down around her neck and over her blouse and sweater. Her skin is delicate, pale and soft, without any wrinkles to betray that she is in her mid-70s.

Her office is hardly decorated other than for what could be called the detritus of an intellectual and academic. Rows of shelves run the length of the wall behind her. The shelves are lined by books with titles such as *Connecting; Family Transitions; Women, Sex and Addiction; Women, Sex and Addiction;* and *Ambiguous Loss.*[1] Near the back-end of the office is her desk with more books piled on it and a photo that I can't quite see. There are more books in her office than I think were in our entire house.

In a corner is a lighted propane fireplace radiating heat. Sitting into the loveseat the room feels warm, cozy, but I still don't know who this person is.

On a table to her side is a small pad of paper and box of tissues.

Dr. Boss picks up the pad and crosses her legs.

"You're going to take notes about me?"

"I'd like to, but I don't have to if it makes you uncomfortable."

"No, that's okay." I settle into the couch and fold my arms across my chest.

"I'll put the pad down for now, but maybe in a bit I'll take some notes."

"Okay."

"So, why don't you tell me a little bit about you?"

"You mean the crash?"

"Why don't you tell me a little about you?"

"Just talk about me you mean?"

"Is that okay?"

"Yeah, everyone else only wants to hear about the crash."

"I think I'd rather hear about you. How are you today?"

Pauline's eyes look straight into mine. They don't waiver. I turn toward the window. "I don't know. I feel sort of lost and invisible."

---

1   Along the spine of this book I read, *By Pauline Boss.*

"Invisible?"

"Yeah…I mean…the crash was horrible…I saw dad and Zach dead and thought mom was burning to death inside the plane after I got out…and everybody treats me like I'm okay…"

"They think you're alright?"

"People just seem to think I'm handling everything and don't really offer much help."

"Help?"

"With trying to, you know, handle the business of death. "

"Okay…"

"And when I see mom…she's so angry at me…all she does is yell at me or make me feel bad when I'm the one who's doing everything. I know she's hurt, and it feels horrible to see everything she's going through, but she's so angry and I'm doing so much."

"Like plan the funeral…"

"Burial. When mom's out of the hospital we'll have a funeral for Zach and dad."

"I would think she appreciates that, you're protecting her…"

I uncross my arms and shift my weight. "…and I'm not just handling the burial. I'm also going to Amery to cancel garbage pickup and take care of the house so it doesn't fall apart. I'm finding and dealing with dad's life insurance, dealing with the will and making sure what he wanted gets done, and all that stuff. There are lawyers calling me, a lot too, and I have to figure out how to pay the bills, lawyers' fees, and all of this financial stuff…"

"Wow, that's a lot, isn't it?"

"…and I've never handled financial stuff before, ever, and I'm meeting dad's financial advisor by myself and holding checks that come in from his work and insurance and I don't know what to do at all. It's all the things that dad would be doing if he could." A tear pushes out from the corner of my eye and Pauline hands me a tissue. "And of course, people are mad at me for not having a funeral now and just having a small—just immediate family—at the burial."

"Who's mad?"

"Some of my family, people at dad's work…"

"You're so young to have to handle all of that …your just 18, right?"

"No, 19…"

"Oh, right…" Pauline looks into my eyes. Her eyes are tender. She's gentle and soft spoken, but direct. "That's still awfully young to be dealing with everything you've had to do…"

"It is, but I'm managing." I wipe my eyes with the tissue. I can't imagine how I must look to her. I'd been out till very late the night before drinking. Before that I'd been with mom in the hospital and we'd argued. When I enter her room, the heart rate monitor ticks up a little bit and she snaps at me no matter what I say. I need to learn to not talk back, to just keep my mouth shut.

"Who are the people helping you?"

"There's my Grandfather and Grandmother Jensen, my dad's parents, but they live in Colorado. Other than that, there really isn't anyone."

"What about your other grandparents, your mother's parents?"

"They're around and do what they can, but it's not much."

"Are they holding you…comforting you?"

"No."

"Why do you think that is?"

"They drink a lot and they've never really been the type of people to reach out to someone and be emotional, or show their emotions. I think they're lost too…kind of dumbfounded by everything that's happened and it's just not their way of living to reach out."

"Even to you?"

"Even to me."

"When I look at you I see a beautiful, young woman…"

"Thank you…"

"…who survived a horrible plane crash, but lost her brother and father, and your mother is so horribly injured…"

"Yeah…"

"…and you're dealing with, you said, *The business of death?*"

"All of the stuff that gets left after someone dies…"

"Alone…or rather, I should say it's slim who is there to help you and be available to you. I think they're well-meaning, wouldn't you say?"

"Yeah…"

"But they aren't there for you in the way you need right now. It probably feels a lot like you're the leader of your family right now?"

"I'm doing what my dad would've done."

"That's a lot for a young woman to do, you know?"

A warm tear courses down my cheek and I quickly wipe it with the back of my hand. "I haven't really cried since getting back from Guatemala."

"No?"

"No, it still seems so unreal that dad and Zach are dead. I've seen their coffins, I know where and when they are going to be buried, but it seems so unreal they're gone."

"You know, you were in that crash too," she pauses and her eyes look down to her notepad then back to me, "you've seen your brother and father dead, their bodies, and your mom nearly burn to death…You've seen things that people in war see; things that affect them for the rest of their lives…"

I nod my head and quickly wipe at my eyes with the back of my hand again.

"It's traumatic; the loss and how horrible it was. Those memories don't disappear, they stay with you, but sometimes they're so horrible we put them away for a little bit because we don't know what to do with them, with the emotions they raise.

"That's okay because everyone grieves and everyone grieves differently. I think maybe we sometimes have to understand that it's okay to be sad, to not be okay. We have to allow ourselves to grieve. It doesn't just happen."

I fold my hands in my lap and look at them; the lines cutting across each knuckle and how white they are. "I don't even know what that means."

"You mean to grieve?"

"What does it look like?"

"Well, that's one of the reasons you're here…to find out."

I lean back and look toward the window. It's overcast outside and cold. Winter is approaching. Pauline is the first person to say, *it's okay to not be okay.*

Pauline and I speak for a few more minutes on grieving and how it's a natural part of how people manage loss, but that after severe loss it can be hard to know how to grieve. On some level I feel like I already know this. It's not as if the word *Grieve* is completely new to me. I watched mom struggle and fight against her emotions after Aunt Vicki died. That's what grieving is to me; fighting against sadness and the sensation of loss.

"You know," she says, "You're allowed to have emotions, and after what you've been through, its okay to let yourself cry."

Yet another tear races down my cheek and I wipe it away. I want to cry, but not in front of her.

Pauline looks into my eyes she says, "With so much going on, what's your life like?"

"What life?"

"Is all of your time taken up with your mom and preparing for the burial?"

"No. After I get up…"

"What time is that, usually?"

"Late, I suppose, around 10 or 11."

"Okay."

"So, after I get up I shower and dress and do all that stuff…"

"Uh huh…"

"…Then I go to the hospital to see mom…"

"Mm hmm…"

"…and mom acts either like I don't exist or yells at me for driving her car around and small things like that. What am I supposed to do?"

"And that makes you feel invisible?"

"And lost. I need her more than ever right now, but she won't even look at me. She looks past me. And when she speaks to me, she snaps at me like everything I do is horrible."

"Does she treat others this way too?"

"No, just me. She's fine with my half-sister Becky and grandma, but she ignores me and is so angry at me…I feel like she blames me."

"For the death of your brother and father?"

"No, for leaving her in the plane…"

"That must be difficult for you."

"It is. I love her and I need her more than ever, but I can't cry on her shoulder, so I pray that she'll get through it someday, that things will get better for us both."

"Your faith is important to you?"

"Very much…I'm not ashamed to love God."

"You don't have to be. Faith in a higher power can be a very good thing."

"All of this had to happen for a reason. It can't just be random that Zach and dad died."

Pauline seems to nod her head in ascent. "You said you need your mom more than ever, but she isn't available to you."

"Yes, but it's not her fault."

"No, it isn't…I didn't mean to infer that it is. Therapy isn't about blame and trying to leave your problems at someone else's feet. You'll get stuck if you go that route, the route of blaming someone, because what happens to you, how you feel and how you heal, depends on you, not that other person."

"What do you mean?"

"You have a mother and you yearn for her, but she's not the mother you want or need right now. She's here, alive, but in the burn unit and not available to you. She's here, but not there for you. This is what's known as ambiguous loss. It's not your fault. It's not her fault. You can't control it. I can't control it."

"Okay."

"If you blame her for how you feel, then you need for her to change, you need her to heal, or at least act in a different way so that you can heal."

"So what do I do?"

Pauline smiles, "Well, that's the confusing part, isn't it? You can understand what's meant by ambiguous loss and that you can't rely on your mom for your own healing, but what do you do with that? It's not an easy question, but it's why you're here, right?"

I look down at my hands. Her question about what my life is like comes back to me. "I go out with friends, too." I feel my cheeks warm.

"How often?"

"Nearly every night."

"What do you do?"

"Mostly hang out and drink."

Pauline's eyes widen, "Do you drink a lot?"

"I don't know…" The memory of the spring semester and how much pain it caused my dad causes my face to redden. "I go to my friends or we go out and drink."

"Do you get drunk most or every time?"

"No," I know I'm being dishonest and look away from Pauline.

"But you drink most nights and always with these friends?"

"Yeah."

"Maybe it helps you cope with everything that's going on around you?"

"Yeah, definitely." It feels safe to let her in this little bit.

"Okay…I think we've done a lot."

"Okay."

"Before you go, I want you to know that I'm immensely impressed by you."

"You are?"

"I am. I think many if not most 19-year-olds would have just thrown in the towel and said I can't deal with this. Instead, as hard as it is, you're dealing with it and probably doing a good job of it for your dad and Zach, as well as your mom. They should be proud."

"Thank you." My eyes moisten, but I hold it in.

"Do me a favor. Think about how much you're drinking and how much of it is to simply numb the pain of all that you've lost, okay?"

"Alright."

"If you need to, call me any time, okay?"

"Okay."

❧≫≪

Leaving Pauline's office I feel lighter than I have in a long time. I am no less depressed or sad or overwhelmed, but speaking with Pauline and letting go, even just a little bit, lessens the emotional weight I carry.

Mom's been in the burn unit for little more than a month. Though she's progressing through one skin graft to the next, eventually to be set free from this very painful way of living, she's still angry with me, she's still physically and emotionally unhealthy.

Meds, constant beeping and blinking lights, pain, colorlessness, unceasing routine, and fatigue disrupt reality for her. She is lucid in most respects, but at any moment veers into hallucinations the nurses call *ICU Psychosis*. The mind can only take so much before it strains against the surreal nature of life in a burn unit.

"There's a cat named Lucy that's been jumping on and off my bed," she said once. I looked around the room wondering how a cat could have found its way into the hospital.

"I don't see it mom."

"What do you mean? It's right here on the bed."

"I don't see it mom."

"Sarah, for goodness sakes its right here…oops, now she's jumped down."

A nurse entered the room, "How are you Mrs. Jensen?"

"There's a cat named Lucy jumping on and off my bed."

"Really? That must be nice for you."

"It kind of is."

The nurse wrapped a blood pressure cuff around mom's arm and pressed a button to start an air pump. Then she placed an electronic thermometer in mom's ear to take her temperature.

"Here's Lucy again," mom said. Her eyes were focused at the end of her bed near her feet. "She's lying down. Maybe she'll go to sleep."

"That would be nice," said the nurse.

Another time mom said she saw an ice cream truck drive out her window. With each hallucination the nurses and other hospital staff simply carry on as if there were a cat named Lucy or an ice cream truck. They aren't fazed one bit by the nature of the hallucinations or their random appearance and mysterious departure. For them, it's normal to live and work in a place where people are taken into a dreamlike state each day. For me, it's disturbing, but a little funny too.

❧❈❦

I pull into a parking space at the hospital after my first appointment with Pauline. It's been about six weeks since the crash. The air outside is cold, even for mid-October. It feels good to enter the warmth of the hospital. In mom's room a familiar nurse goes through the routine of checking her temperature, blood pressure, and querying her about her pain level.

"One to 10, one being barely any pain and 10 being unbearable, where would you rate it?"

"Seven or eight," mom says. It's never more or less. The nurse gives her a little more morphine, or whatever they are using for pain at this point.

"Have you been using the spirometer?" It's a tube with a mouth piece attached used to measure mom's ability to take air in and exercise her lungs.

"Yes," she says, but I don't think she really has. The nurse glances at her sideways, but lets it go.

"Hi mom," I say standing next to her, on her left, away from the cords and hoses.

"You still driving my jeep?"

"Mom, you know I am." Her eyes are drowsy and her lips soft.

"Don't wreck it."

"I won't. How are you?"

"Okay…still in pain." She looks down to her right and lifts her fingers slightly, one after another. Then her eyes move up looking past me to the end of her bed. "There you are."

I look behind me, but no one is there. We're alone in the room. Her eyes flutter and flicker back and forth, as if she's fighting sleep while looking from one face to another. She smiles.

"I've missed you so much," she whispers; then says something that is nothing but a rambling murmur. Then she lifts her hands and begins to speak in sign language to whoever is standing near the end of her bed.

Is it Vicki? Dad? Zachary? I put my hand on my chest, "God, it's them, isn't it?" I know in my heart they're here, they're protecting mom.

I feel it, I feel them. I look back toward the end of the bed and see nothing. Mom continues to sign, pause, giggle and sign.

I feel a mix of helplessness and sadness even as I'm reassured by their presence. I miss them so much and wish I could see them too. The lightness I felt leaving Pauline's office is gone. Zach and dad may be in the air around me, but they can't help me carry any of the burdens of life. Mom continues to smile and mumble and sign. I realize how right Pauline was. Mom is no longer available in the way I need her to be. I have to carry so much on my own.

It's Friday and I know I'll go out with my friends and get very drunk tonight. There's nothing I can do about it. My shoulders sag under the weight of it all.

Chapter 10

Lifting the Veil of Alcohol

*D*ad and Zach were put in the ground on a chilly, but bright day in late September. We are now into late November and a light snow fell during the night. This morning, slate gray clouds give way to wisps of sunlight that soften the snow and dampen the roads. Everything is white or wet.

As I drive mom's jeep to Pauline's, I turn on the radio to block out the early winter sound of rubber tires on cold, damp pavement. It's one of the loneliest sounds that I know.

I'm driving from Uncle Scott's house. About three or four weeks ago he came to me and said "You're staying with me" and that was about it. I didn't have a choice. Later, at the hospital, I looked down at mom, the tubes running from her nose and body, the bandages, the bulge of the colostomy bag on her belly. I don't want his help, or anyone's help; just some indication that they care how I feel, that what happened to mom isn't my fault, that they understand and care I'm in pain too.

"Mom why?"

Mom turned from my eyes, "Just go, Sarah," and I realized I was too tired to fight. The next thing I know, I'm in Uncle Scott's truck driving to the house in Amery to fetch my bed.

After we'd got the bed, he dropped me off at the apartment I was essentially crashing at to pack my stuff. I spent the night and the next morning I drove to his house. He let me in without saying much. I said hi to his roommate, an older guy I'd met maybe once or twice. He tipped his head up at me. Then Uncle Scott led me down a short hallway to the back room and opened the door to a small, cluttered room. In one corner was a gun case, deer heads mounted on the walls, tools in another corner, a worn and beaten desk, my small bed from home with a purple coverlet, and other odds and ends packed in a closet or tucked into a corner or along a wall.

Over the next couple of days Uncle Scott helped me get a waitressing job and life became a tiring daily rotation of visiting mom, work, and once, sometimes twice a week I see Pauline. Three or four nights a week I sleep over at friend's so I can party without having to drive to Scott's. Other nights I drink while listening to music in my room or writing in my journal. It's become a routine that I plan for and look forward to through the day. How to get alcohol, what to get, and then being able to escape into it and away from the hospital, the job, mom, the deer heads, everything.

※※

Though it's nearly 10 am as I drive to Pauline, it feels like very early morning to me. My head pounds and my stomach feels watery from the half bottle of rum I worked through last night. I can still taste it in my mouth, on my tongue; sweet, tangy liquor. Outside, the world is a dull brown making the cold and damp penetrate deeper into my body. Warmth is so far away.

Each of our sessions starts with Pauline asking, *How are you feeling today?* She doesn't push me to tell the story of the crash. I really don't feel up to it. I've run through it so many times when each friend asks to hear it, as if it's some rite of passage for being close to me. I feel numb and respond with a simple, rote story that conveys information without imparting any emotion. It ends with me saying, *Really, I'm okay; its okay,* and then an awkward joke and nervous laughter. Drinking washes away awkwardness, sadness, embarrassment, social unease, but most importantly, the pain I feel deep in my heart. Holding the truth of it in, hiding the emotions and horror the crash truly was, keep my feet moving through each day rather than collapsing into despair.

Pauline seems content to simply listen and empathize that my life must be painful. Every so often she asks questions that dig a bit deeper into the experience or emotion of what I'm describing. She sighs or *Uh hums* in the pauses as I speak and always conveys empathy through the gentle language of her body and soft gaze focused on my eyes. I feel listened to.

The only time she pushes or impels me is when I talk about drinking.

"I still feel so invisible, so numb," I said during our last session a few days ago, "and the people around me don't understand."

"What do you mean?" Pauline asked.

"I still don't cry. I mean, I have cried, but I don't cry when I tell the story or talk about Zach or mom or dad. My friends ask me all the time why I don't cry and are like, 'Why are you laughing?'"

"What do you tell them?"

"I don't know. I guess I just say oh gosh I'm fine, but I'm really not. It feels a-w-k-w-a-r-d, but then someone says something funny and we drink, and, well, off we go."

"Do you spend much time with them when you're not drinking?"

"No, not really. All I do is party, visit mom and then party."

"Does living like this feel okay?"

"I don't know, I mean, it's what friends do, go out and party…it's just what people do."

"No, not everyone."

I crossed my arms over my belly, "Well, where I'm from that's what we do."

Pauline paused and looked down at her notepad for a moment, "I can understand what you're saying. I come from a small town like that too…"

"You did?"

"I did." Pauline shifted a bit in her chair.

"I just mean that you…I don't know, I look at you and I see this totally together person and it just seems odd that someone like you could have come from a place like Amery."

"Professional people come from many different places. I grew up in a small town in Wisconsin, down near Madison. There were probably about 1,200 people in the whole town and my family had a dairy farm."

"Really?"

"Really," she said half smiling. "I was lucky to have two parents who cared about education and were eager to see me go to university, but I wanted to go too." Pauline wiped a bit of lint from her knee. She seemed unsure of how far to let me in to her life.

"So anyway," she continued, "I understand what you're saying that it feels normal to go out and drink like you do, because that's what kids often do in small towns. Sometimes when you've grown up within a family or live in a neighborhood or a certain community where something such as heavy drinking, especially to deal with problems and emotions, is a key part of that culture, you don't know this is not normal until you leave it.

""I suppose this speaks to a type of diversity, too. It's the idea that there are places where people identify with drinking, but not everyone in that community or within even a single family takes part in it. People simply celebrate in different ways."

I sat back into the couch, "Okay." It surprised me that Pauline opened up a little and shared a bit of her life with *me*. Looking at her I would never have guessed she'd seen a cow much less fed one. It wasn't that she exuded only an intellectual, polished demeanor. Far from it, every now and again a word or phrase hinted at something more humble within her. But, I never would have guessed she'd come from beginnings so much more closely connected to the ground, to a rural, farming life.

Pauline seemed so less inaccessible, distant from my own life and experience.

I started talking about my family and how much drinking there is at nearly every single get-together. I described my first year at college and how I fell apart during the spring semester. I told her about being molested by that guy when I was passed out in a friend's dorm room and that just recently I'd been robbed because I was so drunk I could barely function.

I told her I was the first in my family to go to college and how proud dad had been, how unsure mom had been. I told her how horrible it felt to see dad's disappointment when I came home, especially after learning Jacob had cheated on me.

But I also told her how dad still fought for me to go to college. I told her about the alcohol counselor and what I'd learned, but still continued to drink.

Throughout, Pauline listened. Her eyes kept their soft focus on mine and every so often she commented, *That must have been difficult* or *Um hmm* to indicate she was listening and sympathetic.

"Since coming back from Guatemala my life is taking care of mom and then going out and getting drunk with my friends and smoking pot, which I don't even really like how it makes me feel."

"Have your friends said anything to you, what have they noticed?"

"I don't know…I mean, they're drinking and partying too so it's not as if I'm the only person getting drunk and stoned. Like, my friend Emily came to the Cities from Amery and stayed with us for a few days. And I grew up with her and she came to my house every single day during the summers so she knew my family really well, especially Zach, and she's had a really hard time that they died too.

"She's drinking with all of us and getting really drunk and being really promiscuous, so she's not really…I don't know, she isn't really saying anything to me about *my* drinking. My friend Kayla came and visited too and the first time she saw me I was really drunk and I remember her basically laughing at me and said, 'What are you doing?' I think she was more wondering, 'How could you be having fun right now, you just lost your family.' But, you know, I had this it's-all-okay attitude and then she started drinking too.

"So I guess they notice, but then we drink and whatever it is goes away."

When I finished I looked away from Pauline, embarrassed by sharing so much.

She turned her pen in her fingers then said, "I'm scared for you, Sarah. I'm scared for you because the kids in your group get really drunk; so drunk that harm could, and has, come your way. But I'm especially scared for you because it feels like you need to drink like this so often, more than just on a Friday or Saturday night."

"Pretty much every night," I said. I couldn't look directly at her. She wasn't really telling me anything I didn't already know. I know I have a drinking problem. I know I've never really addressed it and by leaving my parents' house, my home, so soon after being rescued by them at college I'd avoided the problem entirely. Dad knew and Zach knew, I'm sure mom knew too, but I didn't do anything about it.

"Sarah, remember when I asked you to think about your drinking and how much of it is to numb your pain?"

"I do."

"You are using alcohol to numb your emotions. It's a dysfunctional way of coping with all that you're going through. Make me a promise, will you?"

"Yes," I said.

"There's an outpatient program that I'd like you to call and go for an evaluation. It's at a place called Hazelden...and I have the number."

Pauline walked to her desk and quickly found the number. She wrote it down on a sticky note and handed it to me.

"I will," I said.

"I'll probably ask you about it at our next session," she said.

"Okay."

❧❦

I arrive at Pauline's office building and step out of the jeep. I've been drinking from a water bottle and feel a bit better, though wobbly. The air smells damp, of decaying leaves and early winter.

I sit in her waiting room for only a short time before Pauline sticks her head out from behind the door and says for me to come in. I go to my usual spot in the peach-colored couch and Pauline settles into her black leather chair. She sets her note pad on her lap and holds her pen in her hands.

"So, how are you feeling?" Pauline asks.

I'm tired from not sleeping very well at Uncle Scott's and I feel guilty for not calling Hazelden. "Not great," I say.

"What's going on?"

"I don't know…I suppose I miss dad and Zach a bit more than usual today."

"What do you miss?"

I focus my mind on Zach for a moment. He's smiling and I feel like I'm going to cry. "I'm really missing being with Zach. I miss us staying up late in his little room talking about everything; school, mom and dad, and just life in general.

"Why do you think you miss him more today?"

"I'm not really happy living with my Uncle Scott." It feels like a copout to lay it all on Uncle Scott. I'm holding back from giving too much.

"It didn't sound like you were very happy there the last time we spoke."

"He's never asked me how I'm doing or if I'm okay. It's like I'm just his roommate. I sound ungrateful and he did help me get a job and it's better than the friend's apartment I was crashing at, but I thought he would be…I don't know…more there for me or something because he took me into his home."

"You feel even more invisible."

"And unwanted, unloved. I mean, not one person in my family— my grandparents, uncles, aunts, cousins—no one has asked how I'm doing. Mom is so messed up and I feel so messed up, but no one's even invited me over for supper. You know, like, 'Sarah, how's it going?' Nobody's done that, but that side of the family never expresses emotions anyway." In the back of my mind I wonder if mom's told them I left her in the plane to burn. Do they hate me too?

"That must be very hard."

"My mom has all of these siblings and nobody's asking if I'm okay… you're the only person who's taken me under their wing."

Pauline shifts in her seat as she hands me a tissue.

I take the tissue and look up at Pauline, "I just want to go home, but I can't. I feel like I don't have a home anymore and I feel so totally, absolutely alone right now."

"When you feel this lonely what do you do?"

"I don't know." I look away from Pauline's eyes, unsure of what to say, my head still aches, my stomach feels sour. "The other night I went out and just sat in the jeep listening to music and when I closed my eyes two images kept appearing…"

"Mm hmm…"

"One was from inside the plane, seeing the front of it crushed down and knowing that's where Zach is. The other is of Zach smiling at me, like a photograph or something…"

"Mm, hmm…"

"And I just missed him so much and was so sad about him…I felt crushed by him being gone and I started bawling my eyes out, really grieving losing him."

Pauline looks at me deeply, intently. I look down at my hands.

"It's so weird, really weird, I guess, but I'm sitting in the car listening to music, bawling my eyes out and I looked into the passenger seat and there's Zach, sitting there, laughing at me."

"Really?"

"Yeah, he's there laughing, having a good time with me. Maybe it was my imagination, or something, but I believe it was him or that God sent that image, that moment because I felt better."

"That sounds like a beautiful moment."

"It was…I almost didn't want to tell you about it."

"Why?"

"God and my faith are really important to me and…" I wipe a wisp of hair from my face. "…I don't know…I don't want you to doubt me or think I'm crazy, but I believe dad and Zach are with God."

"Sarah, I have no reason to doubt you or your faith."

I smile and tell her about my higher power and that I view it as a connection to what I believe is an unknowable God. Then I tell her about mom seeing dad and Zach standing by her bed in the hospital. She listens and smiles.

"Like I said, Sarah, I have no reason to doubt you or your faith." Pauline pauses for a moment then asks, "What else do you do when you feel lonely."

"I've started going to church on Sundays, but I go alone."

"How come?"

"Going to church helps me feel closer to God…"

"Why do you go alone?"

"I tried talking to a couple friends about my spirituality and asked one or two if they wanted to go with me, but they really have no interest."

"What about the people at the church?"

"They're friendly and say hello, but I've kept mostly to myself."

"Why?"

"I don't really feel like I'm someone they'd want to know. They have their families and seem so centered and connected and stable, and I'm the complete opposite of that."

"I think they would welcome you if you let them." Pauline pauses for a moment. "Sarah, have you called Hazelden?"

My eyes wander away from her, "No."

"And you're still drinking, often?"

"Yes."

"And you and your friends are getting very intoxicated?"

"Yes."

"Do you feel safe?"

"No." With each question there is the sting of judgment and criticism, but guilt as well.

"Sarah, you're heading down the wrong path. I'm scared for your safety, but the drinking…well, there is so much good about you and when I hear you saying that the people you see at church wouldn't want to know you, it seems that there is a lot behind that, but first we have to remove alcohol so that we can work on you."

I know she's right. My life to this point has been nothing more than a tug of war between all that I want to be, to become, and the shy girl who doesn't believe in herself. I don't see myself as a good person, a person dad would be proud of. Drinking stops that merry-go-round of feeling inadequate, but it's fleeting and I'm left each morning feeling worse, even more diminished, and less of a strong woman and child of God.

Pauline walks to her desk, finds Hazelden's number. "Please," she says holding it out to me. "You need their help."

I'm exhausted in a way that is deeper than sleep can cure. I'm tired of the struggle, the fight. Each step, each word, each moment feels hard, labored. I'm surrounded by people, but I've never felt lonelier. I long for Zach, for dad. It's an ache, a persistent pain that gnaws at me and wears me down. It saps what resilience I have and I feel my heart, mind and body emptying, becoming even more hollowed out, more numb, than I already am.

I just want it all to stop, I want life to stop, if even for just one moment.

It feels like I'm still in that field. The plane is on fire. I hear mom screaming, *Sarah, please, Sarah, Sarah, Sarah…Oh Sarah…* There is nothing I can do. She's burning and there is nothing I can do to save her, *Please just make it stop, please God, please god, just make it stop.*

Then the face of the man in the field comes to me; his eyes, skin, lips. He handed me his phone, his wife held me and they drove me to a hospital where help, the people who saved mom, could reach us. The image of him, his wife, all of those people rushing past the crumpled body of the pilot toward the blazing plane, risking their lives to do anything they could to help, is so sharp, so vivid that I smell the burning fuel and feel the heat of the flames, the grit of dirt beneath my knees. I see and smell the deep, humid green of the jungle. They had no idea who we were, only that our plane had come hurtling from the sky and crashed in their midst, in their field and probably through their livelihood.

They didn't question the kind of people we were. They offered all they could and I accepted because my need was great. There was so little I could do for myself. I remember Vicki, too. Helpless at the end of her life, but mom and dad gave her so much. They gave her compassion, love, a last moment with her children. Her need was great, but there was so little she could do for herself.

I look at Pauline and I see the same eyes as those people after the crash. I see the same eyes of my parents giving so much to Vicki. I see the same eyes as my dad when I finally came home days before the crash, and I realize my need is great, but I can't do it on my own. I've tried and tried, but I'm worse for it. More than that, I don't care what I have to do to stop drinking, to stop feeling this way, to stop hating myself so much. I don't care what I have to do to ease my pain, to be the woman dad knew I would become…kind, generous, educated, compassionate… to truly be a child of God.

I need help and here it is, reaching out to me, looking at me with kindness, compassion, intellect, committed to those who no longer can manage life on their own. It's the life I want. She is, Pauline, a vision of what my life could be.

My life, I realize, is unmanageable, and it's been that way for a long time. I'll do whatever I have to find the way forward, the path to feeling better, and if it means reaching out for and accepting help and acknowledging I can't do it on my own, I will.

God, all I want is to feel better, to be a better person, to be closer to you…

"Sarah? Why don't you call them right now?"

"Okay." I take the number and pull my cell phone from my pocket.

"My name is Sarah Jensen and I need help," I say to the woman at the other end of the line.

"Can you tell me a bit about what's going on?"

"I've survived a plane crash that killed my dad and brother, my mom nearly burned to death and has spent months in a burn unit, I think I'm an alcoholic, and my life has become completely unmanageable."

"That's a lot," she says.

"It is."

❊❊

I click off the phone and look up at Pauline who's returned to her chair. She's sitting near the edge of the seat, hands on her knees, arms straight, shoulders square.

"Well, it's done," I say. "I go in tomorrow for an evaluation."

"Good, good for you Sarah. How do you feel?"

"I'm ready, I need help and I've known if for a while, but worried."

"About what?"

"I don't know…I mean, everyone I know drinks. It's such a part of my family, my friends and what we do, how we connect…I've already lost so many people."

"Is this something you've thought about before?"

"Yeah, I have."

"Do you think it's kept you from not drinking or dealing with drinking in some way?"

"Yeah…if that's how the people in my life relate, or at least an important part of what they do…it'll just be weird, I mean, I already feel uncomfortable being around my family when they drink the way they do, you know?"

Pauline is very still, "We don't know where all of this is going right now, but the fact that you are looking at your drinking as a problem and that it's unhealthy and not normal represents a cultural shift for you, doesn't it?"

"What do you mean?"

"Well, a few days ago we talked about how drinking the way your friends and family do seems, or seemed, normal to you…"

"Yeah…"

"…there is a strong culture of drinking with them that you've been part of. But now you're questioning that cultural norm and saying maybe it's not normal to drink that way, maybe it's not healthy, and that's a cultural shift for you, your view of the world has shifted."

"Okay…"

"It also means that you may be a little bit on the outside now, and your friends and family may look at you differently, especially with Thanksgiving so close. How do you feel about that?"

"You said I have to deal with drinking so we can work on me?"

"Yes."

"Well, I'm a mess, I'm lost, I don't like myself, and it's not as if they're doing anything for me now."

"What about Thanksgiving?"

"I've never liked how my family drinks so, I don't know, it'll be hard without dad and Zach, and mom in the hospital, but I don't know… it'll be alright."

※※

I walk out of Pauline's office back into the damp cold of early winter. I feel okay. I don't know what it means to say that I have a problem with alcohol, but I feel good about saying it. I feel like if dad could hear me he would be pleased.

When I think of *not* drinking tonight I wonder what I'm going to do. For so long my life has been the business of death. There is still a lot left to do, but much of it is travelling at its own pace, in the hands of others. Today and tonight there are no meetings with lawyers or accountants or funeral directors, or anyone. Even Uncle Scott, in his own obtuse way is making it easy for me to basically do nothing.

I drive to the hospital and walk through the familiar doors and hallways to mom's room where she's been for nearly three months. I walk in and a nurse is checking her pulse. Mom's eyes look away from the nurse, at a point in an imagined far off distance. Though she is depressed, there is also a resilience to mom. I could walk into her room and see her like this, sad, distant, or she could be smiling and sharing something funny with the nurse or a visitor. This is a side of her, social and a desire for life that I've never really seen, other than family parties.

Her attitude toward me rarely changes, she's angry, but she's a bit less harsh, not so sharp with me.

"How are you mom?"

"I'm okay," she says. Her cheeks look pinker and her skin, the skin that wasn't burnt, is less sallow. She's a long way from the ruddy faced woman glowing in the sun while working in the yard, but it's good to see her looking better. She's wearing her wedding ring on a chain around her neck and she starts to turn it with the fingers of her least scarred hand. "I miss my best friend."

"I miss dad too."

"You know it's almost Thanksgiving?"

"I do."

"This'll be the first without them."

"I know, mom."

"People are telling me it should get easier."

"What people?"

"You know, grandma, grandpa, people…but it isn't."

"It isn't for me either."

"It's getting harder."

"What do you mean?"

"It isn't getting easier, it's getting harder because I think they're going to walk through that door any minute and I keep waiting and waiting for them, even though I know they're gone. I just can't stop feeling like they will be here and when they don't walk through that door; it just hurts that much more."

I pluck a tissue from the box near mom's bed and wipe my eyes. I know Zach and dad are dead, and I know that I won't see them again until I die. For mom to have this continuous anticipation that they'll walk through the door any minute, I can't imagine living like that. They're never coming back.

I rub mom's shoulder, but she flinches away from my touch.

"I wish this could just be over," she says.

Chapter 11

Finding Me

*I*t's the second week of December and I'm surrounded by Christmas. I don't think it will ever feel normal to not have Zach and dad in my life, but the decorations, music and celebration of Jesus' birth reminds me that life can be beautiful.

I went for my evaluation at Hazelden three weeks ago. Since then I've been part of their outpatient program for alcoholism, which includes one-on-one counseling and regular *Alcoholics Anonymous* meetings. I haven't had a drink since.

Between the outpatient program, *Alcoholics Anonymous,* and Pauline my life feels as if it's shifted. For the first time in my life I'm among people who are working at improving their lives and being sober rather than merely existing.

I've also started going to a Wednesday night youth group at my new church where there are Bible readings, discussions about God and how

God fits within our lives, and often just to socialize. I'm still nervous to attend, but I feel accepted and that perhaps the work I'm doing to heal myself makes me that much more worthy of their friendship. I feel like less of an outsider.

However, as my circle of friends has grown to include people from *AA* and the church, my other friendships are fading. I still love them, but for now, my life is moving in a different direction. I'd love for them to come with me, but they aren't there yet.

My family has also been a bit of a test. I told them I'm no longer drinking and in conversation I spoke about going to church and *AA*. Pauline was right, they love me still and I love them, but they do look at me differently. It feels as if they're saying, *Oh, Sarah thinks she's better than all of us...* Maybe I'm just reading into how they treat me, but it does feel very different.

I'm still living with Uncle Scott, but mom and I have started talking about living together when she's out of the hospital. She still has a couple more surgeries, but we both see a light at the end of the tunnel and are starting to think about how our lives will work.

Though my life is changing, I still can't get past my grief, which feels sharp and overwhelming. Not to the point where staying sober feels difficult, but the loss of dad and Zach has torn a deep hole into my soul and I don't know how to heal it. Drinking was a temporary salve. Without it, the emotions are more intense and there's nowhere to run and hide, to escape or avoid them. Depression and sorrow are the two most persistent emotions I live with.

❧❦

"How are you feeling today?" Pauline asks after we've taken our normal spots in her office.

"Someone said something to me after an *AA* meeting that made me feel kind of angry at them for having said it, and it's something that other people say to me a lot."

"What was it?"

"'You'll get over it, you just need to find closure.'"

"Why did that make you feel angry?"

"I don't want to get over losing dad and Zach. I don't want it to ever be okay that they died. I'd be turning my back on them, like I'd be forgetting about them and I don't want to just move on like that, without them. I feel like…I feel like I know they are with God, but my sadness, my grief, all of this pain that I'm carrying is the last tangible piece of them that I have. If I let that go, then it feels like I'm letting them go, giving them up."

"Sarah, you've been through a lot, your losses are great, and it's okay to be sad, to mourn for them."

"I know"

"You know, I think this whole thing about closure when it comes to an experience and loss such as yours is really just a myth. How can you find closure on people you have loved and cared about? How can you simply just let go of your feelings of sadness for them? You don't ever get over loss. You learn to live with it.

"So I think that closure is a word that should be used with real-estate deals and business deals, it has no place when we talk about loss and grief. You know, we are one of the only countries in the world that uses it, the term or concept of closure. Many other cultures know that you can live with grief, you don't have to shut the door."

My chest feels tight and I rub my eyes with my hands. "But it's really, really hard to live like this."

"I know, and you don't want to be preoccupied by grief, but its okay to think of them, to remember how they were when they were alive, and to cry over them and feel sadness, that's normal. I also think it's true that when we learn to live with our grief and sadness that we are allowing ourselves to carry the people we've lost with us through our lives."

"I'm scared I won't be able to learn to live with it."

"I think you will. You're doing the work now."

"I suppose that's the difference between mom and me. Mom just recently told me that it's getting harder for her, that she's still waiting for them to come through the door."

"I can imagine her feeling that way."

"Right, but mom grew up in a house where emotions were never expressed and when she married my dad, and especially after he quit meth, he took mom under his wing and really looked after her and helped her be the best person she could be. Without him she's lost, she's not going to reach out for help. She's not going to do this, see a therapist and work through it all.

"I know they aren't coming back and I won't see them again until I pass, and I can't imagine just waiting for them forever."

"Well, it's interesting that there's a paradox here. The more you learn to embrace sadness and grief the less these emotions disable you. I can understand that your mom isn't doing that, isn't hearing what you're trying to share with her. It's hard for you, Sarah, knowing that your mother has a very different style than you and a very different belief system than you have…"

"Yeah…"

"So her way of coping, and perhaps the way she will continue to try and cope with this loss is very different from yours. This is part of what ambiguous loss means. You have a mother, but she isn't quite the mother perhaps you feel you need or that she should be at this time in your life, and she will probably always do it her own way, which is unlike your way."

"Dad would have said that; that I have to learn to accept mom and I are different people, but we can still love each other."

"Well, it's an example of diversity, isn't it? We live in a world of diversity, but sometimes diversity within our own families is the hardest to live with, don't you think?"

Pauline pauses for a moment, looking at me, waiting for a response. "Yeah, I guess."

"There's religious diversity between you and your mother, there's lifestyle diversity, educational level and probably a bit more, but she's a good woman, you've said so yourself and talked to me about how much she showed her love to you and Zach before the crash. But you are different women and it's important for you each to accept the other for how each of you are and will be."

"I wish she could see what I see. I think God, my faith and knowing that I'll see dad and Zach again someday helps me every day. I truly believe I'll see them again, and I wish she could see that."

"I think your desire to help her, to offer her what you have that has helped you so much is part of who you are Sarah. I'm sure she recognizes that, but whether she accepts your beliefs and way of life or not, your mother is your challenge for being able to accept diversity. My mother had an eighth grade education and I have a Ph.D. We couldn't talk about certain things, but we always had great respect and love for each other.

"One thing I would add, because I think it's important to see your differences in order to become closer, to be compassionate, to exercise that emotional muscle we all have, is that you've had a bit of a head start on your mother, haven't you?"

"What do you mean?"

"For so many weeks your mother was in and out of medically induced comas, she's been in surgeries, incredible pain, delusional, living within a burn unit without any break whatsoever, so she isn't as far along as you are in terms of healing emotionally.

"Imagine all that she must have gone through in that plane and then for weeks and months exist in a hospital, constantly operated on and so on. I could imagine she is very tired of the fact that nearly every time someone touches her its to give a shot, wrap her burns, prep her for surgery or in some other way cause her pain even as they are working to treat and heal her.

"She also wasn't able to be at the burial, to see her son and husband placed in the ground. I could never imagine going through what she's experienced, much less expect her to come to terms with it all emotionally, to do the work of emotional healing you've been able to do."

My chest feels tight and I don't feel good about expecting so much from mom. "You mean be a bit easier on mom?"

Pauline nods her head.

I look down at my hands and there's one beat of silence between us. *It's about letting go, opening up.* I look at the skin of my palms; pink, healthy. I open and close my fingers. I remember what mom's legs looked like after we'd made it to the first hospital; the skin taut and stretched to the point where it split like bloated, charred sausage. I remember her screams, how it felt to hear her burn.

I look up at Pauline. Her eyes are soft, lips pressed together. She's been waiting for me to speak. "I remember everything from the crash," the words fall easily from my lips. "I can still feel the emotions, what people were saying, what I was thinking, how fast we were going with the trees whipping by, how scared I was. I remember my dad saying 'Here we go' like we were near the top of a roller coaster about to rush down the track. Mom told him to stop and Zach turned to take a quick look at me, and then there was silence as if everyone, even the plane, is tensing for what's coming. You know the plane is about to hit the ground and you hope it turns out to be okay, but you know it isn't going to be and you wonder if you will be alive in the next moment."

"It must have been horrible."

"I think I closed my eyes just before we touched the ground. Right after that there was a *boom, boom, boom* and then there wasn't any noise at all. I opened my eyes and I realized I was alive, and my butt was supposed to be facing the ground, but it was up in the air and my feet were tucked under my seat. I was dangling upside down with my seatbelt on."

"How did it feel to know you were alive, you survived it?"

"I was just so relieved. Oh yeah, before the plane hit, as we were going down trying to make an emergency landing, I was praying, so I thanked God and thought to myself, *Oh my gosh, I'm alive, everything is fine, we made it.* And I also noticed I'd peed my pants, there was a small cut on my left arm and I was missing a shoe.

"Then I just wanted to get out of the plane. There was a large door right next to me, a big door like you would use to load cargo, and it was open and the sun was shining down onto me, which made me squint. I undid my seatbelt and dropped down onto the roof of the plane and there was broken glass everywhere, like when a windshield breaks. I went out the door and climbed out onto the underside of the wing and we had come down in a field. Just a few feet away, toward the front of the plane, there was a row of palm trees. I looked back and that's when I saw one of the pilots. We'd had a male and female pilot and I think this was the female pilot."

"You couldn't tell?"

"No. She's about ten feet from me and the face is completely bloody and smashed, and I remember his or her legs were twisted up around their head. It was really so sad and disgusting." I look up at Pauline. Her eyes are soft, tender looking. "It was also very hot. So hot it felt like the sun was burning my back. I also remember the smell of what must have been fuel, but it smelled more like diesel to me, kind of like a big truck, an old Caterpillar or Bobcat.

"Seeing the pilot made me realize that things weren't okay and that maybe more people were hurt so I went back into the plane. Mom was hanging by her seatbelt and was just kind of coming to, shaking her head back and forth and trying to work the buckle on the seatbelt, struggling with it. I went to help her, but I couldn't get it to let go no matter how hard I pulled. I thought if I crawled under her I could maybe lift some of her weight off the belt. That's when I saw dad's leg. His side of the plane was completely crushed down and all I could see was his leg up to his knee, and then his boot, just one boot.

"When I saw his leg I started saying, 'Come on dad, let's go dad, dad, dad, come on let's go.' When his leg didn't move at all I realized he's dead, my dad's dead, everybody else is pretty much dead and it's just something I knew. I didn't think that I could help Zach because I just knew my brother didn't make it."

"That's horrible. I'm so sorry." Pauline pulls a tissue from her box, but this time it's for her. She tugs another out and hands it to me. My cheeks are wet with tears; my throat feels tight, dry.

"The silence was eerie. You would think that people would start to talk or that you'd hear something from other people, but it wasn't like that. Other than mom begging me to help her, to get her free, it was completely silent and that silence meant to me that everybody was dead.

"Mom's belt was really stuck because no matter what I did I couldn't get it and she couldn't get it. It felt like there was so much going on, realizing dad is dead, Zach is dead, and now there's the strong smell of gasoline and I see there's fire coming from the front of the plane and it's really starting to come. Mom is getting really frantic and screaming, 'Help me Sarah, help me Sarah, don't let me burn Sarah.' She really, really needed me, but there wasn't anything I could do."

"Oh Sarah…"

"I couldn't think and I didn't know what to do. Then I saw Liz near the front of the plane and she's starting to wake up and hanging upside down like mom. She's moving her head and making noises, sort of mumbling, and I see the fire starting to burn her legs. And just in front of Liz I could see a body. I couldn't tell who it was because the person's head was smashed under the collapsed front of the plane where Zach was.

"Mom's yelling at me not to leave her, but I had to crawl to Liz and try and help her. I couldn't just let her burn, but her seatbelt wouldn't let go either no matter what I did or how hard I pulled.

"I can feel the heat of the fire starting to burn my back, but I can't help Liz, I can't save her, so I go back to mom. I tried to get mom's seatbelt to let go one more time, but it wouldn't. Mom is screaming at me, I was getting really scared and there wasn't anyone coming to help. I was alone and I couldn't do anything for anybody, I couldn't save mom or Liz and dad and Zach are dead. I could hear mom and sparks like when you have a bon fire and the wood pops, and it's getting really smoky and the fire is coming and the airplane is smashed down and I can't see anybody.

"I was so, so scared and thought the plane would explode at any moment and I knew I needed help so I stood up, I needed to get help. And mom is screaming at me, 'You get over here, you get me out of here Sarah, don't you leave, don't let me burn Sarah…' I said, 'Mom, I'll be right back I need to get help, I can't do this on my own.' She's screaming at me as I walked away, but there isn't anything I can do. My God, I felt so worthless, so useless and ashamed."

"You did everything you could." There are tears in her eyes.

"I walked past the dead pilot in the field and the back of the plane is pouring out gasoline. As I walked around the tail there are two men dragging someone from the plane, which I had no idea was even going on, that there was anybody there.

"I tried to go to them, but a man wearing jeans, cowboy boots, cowboy belt, white hat and white shirt, and he is so short, I felt giant compared to him, he sort of appears out of nowhere. I reached out to him and said, 'My mom, my mom, you have to help me get my mom…'

and I tried to push him over to mom, forcing him to the airplane, and I said, 'Help, help my mom.'

"He had a very strong accent, Spanish I think, and he just says, 'No, no, no…' Then he grabbed me and pushed me away as mom is screaming in the background, 'Sarah, help me, help me, I'm burning Sarah, help me…' It was an awful noise and I remember thinking, *Oh my God, my mom is burning, my mom is burning to death right now.* She was screaming for her life and I was numb, I wasn't crying or anything.

"The man sat me down away from the plane and I looked up at him and kept begging him, 'Please, please go get my mom.' He said, 'No, no, no…'

"I'm pleading with him and I can hear mom screaming so loud and about ten or twelve people, men, women and children, surround me and they all put their hands on me and start praying for me. I've never had so many people touching me and saying a prayer out loud.

"Mom is still screaming my name, but also just crying out in pain. She's conscious and burning to death and knows I just walked away… I'm sure that's what she must have thought. My heart is pounding and I can't stop my body from shaking, it was a horrible shaking, and I felt so helpless, so…I can't even put words to how it felt to hear mom burning to death knowing I left her, knowing I couldn't do anything, I was too weak save her. I wrapped my arms around my body to try and stop shaking.

"As soon as the prayer ended, the plane blew up. It was so loud and all of the people who'd been praying stand me up and walk me down a dirt roadway to get away from the plane. I remember the prayer and then a second later, boom, and then it was silence, I don't hear mom any more. All I can see is black smoke rising up high into the sky and there are people, villagers, rushing to the plane. They're running, on bikes, scooters, holding knives; most of them weren't wearing shirts. There was so much going on and so much noise, but I felt like I was wearing earplugs because everything just became so silent. I just became very numb and I couldn't think about anything other than my mom, dad, Zach, my whole entire family is dead."

I continue to tell Pauline my story. I tell her about the man and how his wife comforted me. The drive to the first hospital, how dirty and horrible it was, that I found mom, Liz and Dan there, and then the helicopters. I tell her about the nurse at the second hospital telling me God spared me for a purpose, finding out Liz died, then climbing into another plane with mom in a stretcher to fly home, and how strange it felt to leave without dad and Zach.

There are points where I have to stop because talking about all of this, much of it for the first time, is overwhelming. My voice becomes lost in my tears, my sorrow.

"I'm so sorry you had to go through all of that Sarah. It's a horrific story, but the fact that you're even standing and have done so much to care for your mother and tend to the details of your family, well, I think it's a miracle."

"This is the first time I've told it like that, the whole thing, how it felt."

"How does it feel to have told it?"

"A little better, but it's still so hard. I'd do anything to have dad and Zach back, my mom better, my family the way it was."

"It is a lot of pain and loss to learn to live with."

"It'll never leave me."

"No, it won't. You've been through a lot, more than many people will ever experience. It's okay to be sad, to feel sorrow, but we need to work on you so this experience doesn't prevent you from becoming the woman you're meant to be."

❧❧

Time passes slowly, like an inexorable drum beat, but each day seems to build on the one before.

Telling Pauline my story has not magically *cured* me, but it no longer feels quite so fearful to talk openly and honestly about what I experienced. My early visits to Hazelden were much like those with Pauline, a struggle between my desire to speak freely and my need, perhaps a family legacy, to keep the personal tucked away. I talk about my drinking and the things that happened to me while drunk, but I never share much about what lay beneath the drinking, the emotions, fears, anxieties. That changes, though.

A few nights after sharing my story with Pauline, I eased into it slowly with my outpatient group. There were about 20 people there and it felt hard and uncomfortable to speak about myself and do it so emotionally. I bawled my eyes out, but stuck with it and when I finished I felt a similar sense of relief as I did in Pauline's office.

I wasn't *cured*, but I learned more about trust and it became easier to share with my new group of friends, all of whom are sober and on a journey of faith.

❊

Christmas comes and goes. It's difficult and I still believe that my family's feelings toward me have shifted. Not only am I not drinking, but I'm also attending church regularly, and talking openly about it. I'm not trying to be their evangelist, but I am open and honest about my faith and the new direction my life is moving.

I keep with the Wednesday youth group at church. One night in January, moved by their acceptance, I stand before them and share my story. It is no easier to tell it and I melt emotionally as each memory of losing dad and Zach, mom burning, the bodies I saw passes through me. A few girls cry, the boys listen, almost dewy-eyed. When I finish they tell me how sorry they are, how God must have a plan, and they comfort me in a way alcohol and my other friends never could.

After that night I begin to describe my path to healing as *Soul Searching.* I'm no longer living my life as if I carry my emotions around with me in a box, afraid to untie the string that keeps them held in. Nor am I randomly flailing about looking for anything to distract me from my emotions, from the pain and sadness. I am intentionally seeking transformation. Personal connections in church, *AA,* and especially with Pauline help me feel more at ease. I'm reading the Bible with greater attention to what it and my higher power have to offer for my growing and strengthening faith.

My soul searching is not just about learning how to listen and be closer to my higher power, but includes seeking out who I am and what I want for my life. My sessions with Pauline are extraordinary for helping me, but I'm also reading books such as *Battlefields of the Mind, The Power of Intention, Miracle in the Andes, 90 Minutes in Heaven,* and *Eat Pray Love.* All of them help me look at my life and who I am differently. I no longer see myself as just the lost girl from Amery, but look ahead to what I could become.

Then later in January mom leaves the hospital, finally. She can't drive so I take her to physical therapy appointments and follow up visits with the burn unit doctors. She still has the colostomy bag from her bum being burned so badly and I help her change the bag and clean it each day.

Though I spend so much time with her, we still can't live together. I'm at Uncle Scott's and mom is living with her parents, which is very hard for her. I imagine living with them scratches at old wounds. She's also angry that I can't provide more of her care, but she needs so much that I simply can't do it all on my own. Each day is a new fight with her and it's a very difficult time for us.

"You abandoned me," she says often.

"Mom, I love you, but I can't do it all on my own."

"I wouldn't have to live here; we could live together if you'd do more."

"Mom, I can't…" From there we descend into arguments where all I feel from her is anger, hatred, and frustration with me. She says it's because I won't care for her, that I'm the cause of her living with her parents, her unhappiness, but it's deeper than that.

And she aches for dad, whom she still refers to as *my best friend*. Her heart is broken and life is anything but normal for her. I try to understand that, but she's not the mom I knew before the crash. The affection and subtle demonstrations of love she used to show are gone. She is quick to her anger and I continue to wonder if she blames me for leaving her in the plane. I ask once and she says, "No." It is so flat, angry that I leave it there rather than fight with her about it.

Each Sunday I invite mom to come to church with me, but she says no. After a few tries I stop asking. She isn't into my spirituality; it's a foreign concept to her. It frustrates me, but I learn to be patient and hope that someday she'll want what I've found too.

※※

"How are you today?" Pauline asks. It's early February and bitterly cold outside.

"I'm good. I actually, well, there's someone whose shown some interest in me." I can almost feel my cheeks blush.

"Well, I'm not surprised that a young man would show some interest in you. Is he someone you met at church?"

I smile because I know that Pauline is looking for something, like mom used to do, to protect me. "He's part of a group of friends that I've met through my work."

"So he's not part of the group you drank with?"

"No, he's a really nice guy. Probably drinks socially, but, I don't know, he seems like a really nice guy."

"How do you feel about the possibility of a relationship?"

"With him, or you mean in general?"

"Both, I suppose."

"I do like him, he's nice, his name's Adam, you know, first name in the Bible. I don't really feel ready for a relationship, but I guess I worry, what if I miss out on being with a really great guy if I say no to him?"

"If you aren't ready don't you think you should honor that, for him and you?"

"I know. Who's to say what's going to happen, relationships can be complicated, but I still worry if I say no to him."

"Why does it have to be either or?"

"What do you mean?"

"Why does it have to be a relationship or not right now?"

"You mean take it slow?"

"Why not allow the friendship to grow and see where that leads you?"

"I guess I don't have to close the door. I can leave it open, but work on being friends for now."

"Yes, after all who's in charge of your life, your decisions?"

"I am, so I can move at my own speed, make my own decisions." I look at Pauline, "My dad would have said pretty much what you said, 'Be in charge, responsible of your own life.'"

"It's less an order than it is that you recognize your decisions are yours and you can move through things such as relationships at your own speed, weigh the options and so on, rather than letting others influence what you do."

"I don't think dad ordered me to be in charge of my own life as much as it was something he wanted to see me do. A wish he had for me."

"I see. It was more about compassion and his hopes for you than anything else?"

"That's who he was. He was such a good man. He'd do anything for anybody. He loved being able to do that, to help people, and I think it really frustrated him that I never seemed to ask for or take his help, even though he offered it all the time."

"What do you think kept you from being more open to him?"

"I always took what he said as criticism, that I wasn't good enough or making the right choices or doing the right things or dating the right guy…that I was a mess."

"What would he say to you now?"

"I wish he could see what I've been doing, to know I'm okay."

"He would say he's proud of you?" Pauline shifts slightly in her chair.

"I think so, and that he wishes I'd go back to college."

"Why?"

"Because he believed I needed a college education to have a future and that I was smart and had something to offer the world and that college would let me do that."

"You mentioned the nurse in Guatemala saying God spared you for a reason, that there's a purpose. What do you think that is?"

"I'm not sure, but I've been thinking about that, what am I supposed to do, how am I supposed to live up to this gift God gave me?"

"What do you think?"

"I've seen so much compassion towards me, from the help of those people in Guatemala to the church and my friends, to you, and no one's expected anything in return for it. They just gave it. I'd like to do that, to be who you've been to me, to be able to understand how to help someone who's as lost as I've been. I've been a self-centered person for too long and I don't want to be that way anymore."

"Someone once told me that empathy and sympathy, the emotions that allow some people to be so giving and forgiving toward others, are like muscles. Everyone has them, but they need to learn how to use them and exercise them regularly for them to be strong. I think you could grow to be very strong, I think in many ways you already are."

"Thank you."

"So if your purpose in life is to help people, how do you think you want to do that?"

"I want to go back to school."

"I think that's a beautiful way to honor you father and live your life's purpose."

I tuck a loose strand of hair behind my ear. I feel as if I've been on a very long climb. "I've always wanted to go to St. Catherine's here in The Cities," I say almost as if it were a question.

"Listen," she says, "let's do something a bit different. Let's get out of this office and visit St. Catherine's as one of our sessions."

"Together?"

"Yes, together, but rather than presenting me as your therapist I would just be a friend of the family, maybe a mentor."

❄❄

A month later I'm with Pauline in the admissions office speaking with an admissions counselor. She explains that the school is all about self-reflection and growth. You don't go there to sit in a classroom with a hundred people and learn what you are going to be taught for the day. Instead, you are in smaller classrooms with only a few people and talk about yourself, the people in your life and your experiences. You talk about how all of that fits together to create who you are and how you will use that to become and succeed as a professional woman.

Of course, this is done within the context of a curriculum that encourages critical thinking, discussion, personal responsibility, intellectual curiosity, and independent thinking.

The counselor also describes why St. Catherine's remains an all-girls school, its liberal arts and Catholic intellectual mission, and then a bit about financial aid and grants that could be available if I decide to go there. As we run through all of this I think, *Oh my God, I can't believe I may actually be able to do this, to live this life, to be part of this school.* I felt, for the first time in a very long time, if not ever, that I know what I want to be in a way that helps define who I am, and that I'm actually taking steps to move forward instead of just talking about it.

I look at Pauline and she smiles back. She seems proud of me and I'm glad for it, but wish too that I could share this with mom. I love her and miss her and need her support, for her to be proud of me, but also I think she needs this in her life too. If I finally have a vision of a future that I want, that makes me feel so good, I wish mom could have this same experience.

And I think of Zach and dad. Zach would have been happy for me, dad would have been so proud of this.

"Do you have any questions before we go on the tour?" the counselor asks. She and Pauline look at me and I feel a bit intimidated by these women. Though I feel better, I still carry the old self-doubts, especially in the presence of these accomplished women.

It's hard asking, but I have to, "My first college experience didn't go so well…" and then I describe failing out of the University of Minnesota at Duluth. Without giving too much detail I describe struggling with school and that I hadn't been ready for the challenge of it, of dealing with life on my own, without my family right there. I also tell her that I've been through a lot, the crash and all of the soul searching and work I've done and continue to do to move forward in my life, and I tell her that that college, St. Catherine is part of that.

At first her eyes don't betray any emotion, any connection to my story, but then she looks into my eyes, "I'm so sorry you've had to go through all of that. I think what's important is to first make the decision that St. Catherine's is right for you. If it is, if we're the right fit for each other, I'm sure we can find a way. We are looking for young women who want to develop into strong, confident women who carry themselves in the world with empathy and sympathy and intellect. It seems that this may be you, so we'll try to work with you."

"Okay," I say as I wipe a tear from my eye. Acceptance is such an incredibly powerful thing.

As we walk through the campus I imagine that my mouth hangs open in awe the entire time. My body feels as if it's shaking with impatience. I want to be here now. Then we walk to the campus chapel. It's a large, church and bell tower made of granite blocks. Inside, it's beautiful. The walls are the same sandy fawn colored stone with row after row of aged wood pews leading to the apse, which has a small, yet beautiful blue stained glass window near the arch of the half-dome above the alter. Running along either side of the pews are Doric pillars supporting arches that in turn support the domed ceiling. Windows run along the exterior walls, which allow light to nearly flood in.

It's absolutely beautiful. *This would be on my campus?* I think to myself. *I could just come here any time and pray and talk to dad and Zach and be alone?*

"…and this is open to all of our students any time they need or want what they can find here…" She says.

"You look like you're in awe," Pauline says.

"I'm ready," I said looking at the counselor and Pauline. "This is what I want, where I can become the woman I want to be."

❧❦

Over the next few weeks Pauline and I continue to work on adjusting to a life living with the sadness and grief of loss rather than collapse under its weight. Pauline helps me with the application to St. Catherine's and even writes a letter of recommendation for me.

I also speak to mom about going. Initially, she questions whether this is a good idea and if it's something I could actually succeed at. Underneath, there's anger and disappointment in me. Perhaps she feels me pulling further from her, threatened that my life is moving forward while she feels stuck, living with pain and unable to come to terms with losing dad and Zach, always waiting for the door to open.

But she's also conflicted, I think. It's hard to believe she's lost the desire to see her daughter do well, her love for me. It's there, beneath all of the crap, but it's there. It has to be.

She cautiously agrees with my desire to go to St. Catherine. I don't need her to say yes, I could go anyway, but I want it, I need her support, I thirst for the smallest signs that she loves me, accepts me, wants me. I suppose she wants as much from me.

"I love you mom."

She looks at me. For a moment there storm in her eyes subsides, there's calm, "I love you too honey."

I send the application and all that's left is the waiting.

"How do you feel today, Sarah?" Pauline asks. It's early April and the first, earliest hints of spring are poking through the earth or in small green buds on a few trees. It's still chilly, but the weather is more like a difficult, emotionally volatile companion, warm one day, cold and rainy the next.

"Pins and needles, I'm on pins and needles."

"So I suppose you haven't heard from St. Catherine yet?"

"No, it'll be a few weeks, but I can't wait."

"Me too," Pauline smiles, "but I think you've got a good chance." Pauline pauses for a beat, tilts her head and presses her lips together, then asks, "How's your mother?"

"She's doing better," I say frowning a little bit.

Pauline's head seems to nod in recognition of what I'm feeling. "There's something I want to share with you."

"Yeah?"

"Your mom called and spoke to me briefly about you."

I cross my arms over my chest. "What'd she say?"

"Well, we said hello and introduced ourselves to each other and then she mentioned you had spoken to her about St. Catherine. I told her that you would like to go there, which she knew, of course. Then she said, and I thought very sincerely, that she is glad I'm helping you go in that direction because she can't right now. I was very moved by what she said.

"Your mom also said, 'I can't help her get in there, but I'm grateful that you are able to encourage her to go to college because that's what her dad and I wanted so much for her, to see her do that and succeed.' I was very touched by that, too."

"Why can't she share that with me?"

"I don't know, but I think she's trying. Remember when we talked about not drinking being a cultural shift for you?"

"I do."

"Well, reaching out and sharing her emotions is a cultural shift for her. I think it's important to recognize that, to value that she's trying."

"I haven't seen any of it."

"Maybe it's there, but you need to be better at seeing it."

"Maybe." The tension in my arms eases and I look at Pauline, "We also spoke about diversity."

"I remember," Pauline says sitting back in her chair.

"And I thought of it as I have to live with how she's different from me, but I think I also have to see how I'm different from her and what that means.

"I want a much different life from hers. I want academics, college, and an intellectual and professional life instead of waking up each day before the sun and wandering to a menial job I don't like. I don't want to drink, or at least not have it be the center of my life, and I want to be more than I am now.

"I suppose if I were my mom, I would feel hurt that my daughter is rejecting my life, rejecting me, and that's gotta be even harder with dad and Zach gone."

"As a mom, I would add there's another piece to that. It hurts to have to so thoroughly let go of not just a husband and son, but a daughter as well, even if you are proud of what she may be able to accomplish, she still has to let go of you. It's an ambiguous loss for her, isn't it?"

"She needs me to be something for her that I can't be."

Pauline nods.

I look out the window, "I had a dream the other night."

"Oh yeah…"

"In Amery we lived near a river, the Apple River, and Zach and dad and mom and I would swim there during the summer. Probably Zach and I more than mom and dad, but when he went, dad loved the water and mom usually sat on the bank watching. In the dream I'm riding on dad's back, sort of floating together with me holding onto his back, and we're in the water because we were all in a plane that crashed into the Apple River, but we're okay.

"It's just dad and Zach in the dream. And dad's shirt is off and he has huge tattoos all over his back. So he's giving me sort of a piggy back ride and we're in the water, splashing and having fun. I could feel him. I could feel Zach near me and I could hear them talk and laugh and tell me how much they love me and I told them how much I love them.

"Then I woke up, but I felt happy that they came to visit me in my dream. I was safe, protected. I missed them terribly for the rest of the day, but the sensation of having been with them and how good it felt stayed with me."

Pauline looks down at her hands for a moment and then to me. Her eyes are soft and voice nearly a whisper, "Even though your father is dead he's helped save you because he created such a positive desire in you to be a better person, to go to college and make a good life for yourself, one where you could be happy.

"That's the transformation that is so unique that you have made; that transformation of meaning, the meaning of what happened to you. You have transformed it into something positive that moves you forward in a very healthy and strong and wonderful way so that you'll make a contribution to society.

"You could still be wailing about this terrible loss of your father and brother and of course you still feel that sorrow, longing for them, but you have this stronger feeling that the wind is behind you. That's the transformation to resilience, which is so wonderful, so unique. Not everybody does that. Not everyone can do that.

"There's more to do, but you really are living your life in a way that honors your father. I know he'd be so proud of you."

I wipe my eyes. I know dad and Zach with me, and I feel mom's love. There are tears in Pauline's eyes too. "I guess what I've learned is if you don't do the work to move forward, to attempt to start life over, you may miss the opportunity to see that life is beautiful."

Epilogue

I often wonder to myself, "Why did this happen to me? Why did I have to lose my family when I was only 19? God, how could you do this to me?" Did I possibly do something to bring this curse upon myself?

Or, was my dad and brother's lives simply complete and they were destined to heaven far sooner than I can understand?

The thing is, I will never understand.

I also often wonder where I would be today if it weren't for the accident. Would Zachary have gone to college or into the military? Would dad still make log furniture? Would I be living at home with my parents, drinking myself deeper into a depression? I don't know, but I do know my life has been a work in progress beginning even before August of 2008.

Today, more than ever, I am truly grateful. I have a wonderful husband, two children, and a home to call my own. I'm in graduate school working towards becoming a marriage and family therapist. And, I live my life as a true Child of God. My journey has not been easy, but it has been worth it. I'm destined to live a life of happiness and joy because a true intervention happened that day in August, a Divine Intervention to stop the cycle of alcoholism and depression I'd fallen into.

Adam told me after we started dating, "The moment I saw you, I knew I was going to marry you." I never had that *fell in love at first sight* feeling, but I did have a moment with my Higher Power late one night. He told me to call Adam and that he truly is meant to be my husband. Thankfully, I listened to God and on September 1, 2012, Adam and I were married.

Our marriage is not always as easy as perhaps one would hope. After all, I have my past traumas that get in my way and Adam has his own past traumas that get in his way. But one thing that we do know is that we love each other. We both know God arranged our meeting and we are destined to be together. We never lose sight of each other, and when things get tough, which they do, we always resort back to the love that is the granite-like foundation of our marriage. I've learned apologizing goes a long way, and I always want to be better, for Adam and our children.

We have two children, Lillian and William. I honestly never thought of myself as a mother while I was growing up. I knew I wanted to be married, but kids, whoa, that was a far idea for me. But now I have them and they are beautiful. Any parent knows that there are no words to describe what being a parent feels like; it is simply a deep and enduring blessing.

While my time at the University of Minnesota-Duluth was a low point in my life, attending St. Catherine University is a foundation of my intellectual, spiritual and emotional growth. I failed out of Duluth, but graduated from St. Catherine's with a 3.8 GPA and a BS in Social Work. I worked, I studied, I dedicated my time to my academics and did so not just to prove something to me or my professors, but to honor my dad as well. It was his inspiration that kept the drive alive in me. Dad knew I could do well in school, and I was going to prove it to him and myself. And I did, and continue to do so.

Today, I've continued with my education and am working toward my master's in marriage and family therapy. This, in part, is due to the work that I did with Pauline. She is more than simply my therapist. She believed in me even when I couldn't.

She saw things in me that I didn't see in myself. She saw what dad saw, and that saved me from going in a different, far darker direction. I could've easily lost sight of my gifts and fallen further into depression, anger, and alcoholism. But I didn't. Pauline helped me see that I'm capable of living the life I want and dream of. She showed me I was strong enough to do it on my own.

Pauline advocated for my personal growth, my academic growth, and my spiritual growth. She guided me in the right direction, and because of her, I am truly thankful. God puts people in your life for a reason, and I think He put Pauline there, when I had nobody else during that difficult time.

Why I wrote this book?

I have lived a life of loss, depression, alcoholism, even emotional abandonment, but I have survived it. I am slowly beating it. And now, I want to use my adversities and experiences to help those who need it the most. Those who are struggling to see the light. I can give back to my clients what I experienced in therapy. I can, and I will. I am destined for this profession, and I am grateful to know this.

Although it may seem that I have everything together and my life is *perfect* it is far from such a thing. I have my continuous ups and downs that affect not just my mood, but my personal relationships and my relationship with God.

Since the accident, the loss of my dad and brother is concrete. I know they have passed on into the spiritual world, and when I pass, I will be reunited with them again. There is another loss that I have struggled to acknowledge and understand. That loss is with mom. Although mom and I live next to each other, we are far from being close neighbors. We live our own lives and have a very emotionally detached relationship. We live two very different lives. I know we are in different places in our lives right now, but this emotional detachment I experience day in and day out has taken such a toll on me. I am hurt. Since the accident, my mom has chosen a different way of grieving; or lack of. This lack of grieving has essentially put an invisible fence between the two of us. We both see the world differently.

I have tried and tried to get my mom into therapy. She refuses. I so desperately want my mother to cry and release the pain she carries so she can attempt to start a new life, one where she is at peace with the loss of her son and the man she describes as her best friend. I wish this for her and pray for it so she can see the true beauty life has to offer, what God has to offer. Someone once told me to "let her go." But the thing is, I can't. I can't let go of my mom. What I can do is forgive. Forgive not only who my mom is, but forgive myself. Forgive myself for leaving her in the airplane that day. Forgive myself for letting go of her in the first place. Forgive myself for almost allowing her to burn to death. Once I learn to forgive myself for the pain I have caused my mom, for walking away that day, then I won't feel I *owe* her something. I hope someday mom has the strength to forgive me…

I never grew up in a religious family, but I always wanted to know God. His seed was planted inside me from such a young age. Then, that night in Duluth with Jacob changed my life. Seeing God's light was the best thing to ever happen to me. Not only did it start a relationship between God and I, but it changed my views on life. I often wonder why God showed Himself to me that night. Maybe it's because He wanted to show that I too could influence the life of even just one person. What if my story changes the way a person thinks about God or even the way he or she lives her life? I can share my story with you while others may not have the opportunity to do so.

My relationship with my Higher Power has had its ups and downs, just like any relationship. I go to Him when I need Him, I stray when I am feeling confident and happy. When I start to feel I need him, I go back. It is a continuous cycle, and more recently, I have learned I always need God. Through not only the bad times, but the good as well.

After I had my son William, Adam noticed I was having another episode of post-partum depression (Yes, I struggled with post-partum depression after I had my daughter). I was just sad. Anybody who has ever struggled with post-partum depression knows what I am talking about. Having a new baby, taking care of a toddler, juggling school and my house, all while being depressed is not fun. But, he convinced me to get back into the gym and take care of myself. And I did.

On this *taking care of myself* quest, not only was I working out at the gym, but I also started reading again. I started praying again. God is never more than a prayer away, and I feel his love when I seek Him out. He is always with us, whether we realize it or not.

When one door closes, another one opens. Throughout this journey, I have not only lost loved ones, family, and friends, but I have also gained new family, new relationships with friends, and a new relationship with myself. My whole life growing up, I never truly knew my half-sister, Becky. We are seven years apart, so the significant age difference not only stood between us, but we were raised totally differently too (that's another story). After the accident, Becky went from not being in my life, to being there every single day. She, and her husband Chad, were at my mom's bedside every day. She fed my mom, she helped changed bandages for my mom, she was moral support for my mom. Becky was there for my mom, not only physically, but emotionally, when I couldn't be. And for that, I give my greatest gratitude.

Today, Becky and I are slowly developing our relationship. Although we are sisters, just like any relationship, one must start slow. And, that's what we have done. We have slowly begun being sisters for the first time in our entire lives. It makes me so happy. I know dad and Zach would also be happy.

One lesson in particular that I have learned is, I don't have the power to change other people. I can only change myself. I can change my way of thinking, I can change how to seek happiness, and I have learned that nobody can make me happy but myself. This is a slow journey, through prayer and continuous spiritual growth. I have come to this realization. Happiness is within. Our power is within. Instead of looking outward to find completion or happiness, whatever you call it, we need to look within ourselves. God has given us whatever we need to survive the adversities, the obstacles that Earth provides. Once we can acknowledge that we have the strength to change then we can move forward with our lives. The world will look so differently. You start to notice little things that you never noticed before; inside yourself and outside in the world.

Martin Lawrence once said, "Nobody is immune to the trials and tribulations of life." That quote has stuck with me ever since I heard it. It is true. We all have adversities, we all get stuck, but we all have the power to move forward with our lives.

If you do the hard work today, you will have Joy later. And that Joy is amazing. It is Bliss. It brings you closer to your Higher Power. You know you're doing the right thing. Life is beautiful, why not enjoy it?

Acknowledgements

First of all, I want to thank God for giving me a second chance at life. I am forever indebted and will always strive to be like You.

Adam, I love you. Thank you for being patient with me and always supporting me. I know I have not been easy, but I promise you, it will be worth it. You are my rock.

I am incredibly grateful for Dr. Pauline Boss for always being there for me. Thank you for believing in me and pushing me to be the best person I possibly can be.

James, without you, this book wouldn't be possible. Words can't describe how appreciative I am for you and our work together.

And finally, during my most vulnerable moments, prayers were still sent my way. Thank you for those who prayed, who donated, and who helped my mom and I get back on our feet, when we needed it the most.

I would like to acknowledge all the lives lost aboard our airplane and for their families who suffered; Roger Jensen, Zachary Jensen, Cody Odekirk, Jeffrey Reppe, John Carter, Lizabeth Johnson, Lydia Silva, Louis Javier Rabanales, and Walfred Rabanales, the pilot Monica Bonilla, and co-pilot Fernando Estrada.

About
the Author

Sarah Johnson is a graduate student working to be a Licensed Marriage and Family Therapist. She wants to specialize in working with those who have lost loved ones and are having a difficult time with their grieving process.

Sarah lives in Minnesota with her husband and two children.

www.lifeisbeautifulbook.com